Barney Fife and Other Characters I have Known

Don Knotts

with

Robert Metz

Barney Fife and Other Characters I Have Known

BERKLEY BOULEVARD BOOKS, NEW YORK

All interior photos courtesy the author's personal collection except those appearing on pages 107, 176 courtesy Twentieth Century Fox; pages 111, 113, 114, 115, 120 courtesy Viacom; pages 137, 139, 140, 142, 144 courtesy Warner Bros.; pages 146, 149, 156, 159, 160, 164, 165, 166, 167, 168, 173, 175, 178 courtesy Universal; pages 196, 200 courtesy Walt Disney Studios; pages 203, 204, 206, 207 courtesy DTI.

BARNEY FIFE AND OTHER CHARACTERS I HAVE KNOWN

A Berkley Boulevard Book / published by arrangement with the authors

PRINTING HISTORY
Berkley Boulevard trade paperback edition / November 1999

The Penguin Putnam Inc. World Wide Web site address is
http://www.penguinputnam.com

ISBN: 0-425-17159-0

BERKLEY BOULEVARD
Berkley Boulevard Books are published by The Berkley Publishing Group, a division of Penguin Putnam Inc., 375 Hudson Street, New York, New York 10014. BERKLEY BOULEVARD and its logo are trademarks belonging to Penguin Putnam Inc.

PRINTED IN THE UNITED STATES OF AMERICA

10 9 8 7 6 5 4 3 2

Foreword

Don Knotts's full name is Jesse Donald Knotts. I met him the second day of rehearsals for the Broadway play *No Time for Sergeants*. Here's how it happened:

There used to be a radio show called *Bobby Benson and the B-Bar-B*. Of course it was a western and it had Bobby, the kid; Tex, the foreman of the ranch; an Indian; and an old man named Windy Wales who told tall tales. I used to listen to it as I drove from job to job. That rehearsal for *No Time for Sergeants* I mentioned started with a preacher walking onto the stage to introduce my character, Will Stockdale. Don played the part of the preacher speaking as an old man. After he finished, I said, "Excuse me, aren't you Windy Wales?" He was. And that's how I met Jesse Donald Knotts.

Don was not in the pilot for the old *Andy Griffith Show*. But when he saw it, he called me, and said, "Don't you need a deputy?" That phone call made all the difference. In the beginning, the idea was that I would be funny. It didn't take any time at all to recognize that Don should be funny and that I should play straight for him. I want you to know the truth. That is what made the show so popular.

Don was not Barney Fife. Barney Fife was a character that Don created. I know Don to be a bright man and very much in control of himself. As everyone knows, Barney Fife had very little control of himself. In the comedy scenes we did, I was often closer to Don than the camera and I could look at him before we started those scenes, and through his eyes, I could see him become Barney Fife. I am certain that I will never have again an experience as joyful and fulfilling as that one with Don.

Jesse Donald Knotts is a brilliant comic actor. He would be able to do any kind of acting, but he'll probably never get the chance because he is so gifted at comedy.

—Andy Griffith

The House on University Avenue

My ambition to become an actor goes as far back as I can remember. I was so committed, in fact, that the possibility of becoming something else never even occurred to me. I suppose it all started with my mother. She was a devoted movie fan and she started taking me to the movies along about the time that talking pictures were coming in. I must have been about five years old. Laurel and Hardy and Abbott and Costello soon became my favorite funny men. Like so many of my peers, my idol on the radio was Jack Benny. It was a dream come true, some thirty years later, when I shared the stage with Mr. Benny on a television special on CBS.

I grew up in Morgantown, West Virginia, in the 1930s. I lived with my mother and father, along with my two much older brothers (they were teenagers when I was born) in a big old house on University Avenue near the campus of West Virginia University. My father, who had suffered a severe nervous breakdown and physical collapse shortly before I was born, was now, for the most part, bedridden. My mother supported us by renting out rooms and cooking for college students. Frustrated by the De-

My mother

pression, my brothers, already young men, could help out only occasionally when they picked up temporary work.

My mother and father and I occupied the two main rooms in the house, the living room and the kitchen. Mom and Dad slept in the living room, and I slept on a daybed in the kitchen. Sid and Shadow shared a bedroom with our star boarder, Tom Helfrik. Tom, a WPA foreman and the only employed person in the house, lived with us for many years and was considered part of the family. The reason for all this doubling up was to leave the remaining four rooms free for rental. I had a third brother, Bill, who did have a steady job, but he had his own family to support. A store manager for Montgomery Ward, he was frequently moved from one town to another. Bill helped us out when he could. He and his wife, Hazel, and their first son, Don (named after me, I was told), came to visit us once or twice a year, usually bearing gifts. Sometimes during summer vacation, they would take me with them to spend a couple of weeks. I looked forward to those visits. I was much in awe of my successful brother Bill.

Financial help from Bill, whenever he could help us, was probably about all that saved us. Keeping the rooms rented and then collecting the rent when they were kept my mother in a constant state of worry. I remember one month she had to sell her upright piano, which she had dearly loved to play, in order to pay *our* rent. These were tough times. It always seemed that we were right on the verge of going "over the hill to the poorhouse," as the expression went in those days. Moss Hart once wrote, "The poorhouse wasn't bad enough. They had to put a hill in front of it."

It was my father's illness that had led to our financial woes. My father and mother had both been farmers and after they were married, my father purchased a farm a few miles outside Morgantown where all three of my brothers were born. My father was a hard worker. In addition to the backbreaking work of farming, he found time to do some small-scale mining of coal that he found on his land.

One day, my father was led home from the field unable to see. He lay in bed blind for two weeks. He got his sight back and never lost it again, but his health, both mental and physical, began to fail. Soon he was unable to continue working the farm. Shortly before I was born, he lost it and moved the family into Morgantown. For a while, my father tried to make ends meet by selling real estate, but his health was gradually deteriorating and before long, he was hardly able to work at all. Within three years or so, we were flat broke.

It was then that my mother, in desperation, decided to lease the big house on University Avenue and rent out rooms to students. By this time, my father was in bed as much as he was out. Once a strong, vibrant man, a successful farmer and an elder in his church, my father lay anguished in his bed in our living room. Paradoxically, at times he would get out of bed and become violent. Twice he threatened Mom with a knife and was confined briefly to the state mental hospital near Morgantown. They more or less warehoused mental patients then. He got almost no therapy. There were no mood stabilizers, no Elavil, no Prozac. I'm confident that in today's world my father would have been treated for psychotic depression. Modern medicine might have had him on his feet and active, getting on with his life. But for as long as I can recall, my father rarely got out of his bed.

Shadow and the Family Humor

The trait that served my family best was a sense of humor. Despite our somewhat desperate circumstances, there was always laughter in our house. Both Sid and Shadow were funny, but Shadow, in particular, was a natural, gifted comedian, and he couldn't have asked for a better audience than my mother and me. My mother loved to laugh and he could send me into waves of hysteria. When I was little, I would follow him around the house encouraging his antics with gales of laughter. He brought great joy into my life. I remember how sad I would feel when he would leave the house, and I would escape the gloom that sometimes pervaded our house in those early days by filling my space with imaginary characters with whom I would act out some happy drama. I suppose it's quite possible that this was the true beginning of my acting career. Shadow certainly kindled the spark of the comedic in me, there is little question about that.

Shadow's sense of the ridiculous was somewhat astonishing, considering the fact that he was in terribly poor health. He suffered from asthma so severe that he often had to sleep sitting up, and he was frequently plagued with lung infections. Six feet tall, Shadow stood as straight as a soldier at attention, but he was as skinny as a rail, thus inspiring the nickname Shadow. His real name was William Earl. My mother called him Earl. Brother Bill's real name was Willis and Sid's real name was Ralph. My mother insisted on calling all my brothers by their real names. She was the only one who did. She called me Donald.

Shadow's humor included poking fun at his own skinny frame and ill health. When he took his physical examination for the army at the outbreak of World War II, he insisted that the

My brother Shadow

doctor had written "fit as a fiddle" on his examination results. Once when he was sick in bed, I asked him what was wrong with him. He looked up at me weakly, and said, "Everything I eat goes to my stomach."

The dinner hour was usually filled with laughter. Our kitchen was quite large and in addition to the kitchen cabinet, stove, and ice box, it accommodated my daybed and a large old-fashioned round dinner table.

Typically seated at dinner would be my father and mother, Sid and Shadow, Tom Helfrik, and probably one of the other boarders and myself. The clowning would begin with Shadow buttering his bread as if it were a violin, tucking it under his chin and using the butter knife for a bow. It might continue with Shadow commenting to Sid under his breath, but loud enough for all to hear, that poor Tom Helfrik had had two helpings of meat already. Sometimes the dinner hour would become complete mayhem, and I would laugh so hard I would have to leave the table, and the tears would run down the cheeks of my dear mother.

It's interesting that my father usually found the strength to get out of bed and come to the dinner table, but he did not join in the fun. He had no reaction at all to the clowning and laughter that went on around him. He seldom spoke and when he was finished eating, he simply rose and walked stiffly back to his bed. One evening he did speak, however, and he cracked us all up. The *Amos 'n' Andy* comedy show was easily the most popular radio program in America during the '30s. We were discussing the show at dinner, reciting lines that had made us laugh. When people spoke of the team of Amos and Andy, they usually pronounced it as if it was one word: Amos'n'Andy. Well, in the midst of our discussion of the *Amos 'n' Andy* show that evening, my father suddenly broke his silence and yelled, "I'm sick and tired of hearing about this Andy and Amos." Well, we howled.

Drunk and Disorderly

In addition to taking care of my father and overseeing my upbringing, my mother had her hands full with the sometimes rowdy college students who occupied our rooms. College students were pretty wild in those days, and they could get pretty drunk and disorderly sometimes. They built themselves such a bad reputation, in fact, that local residents tended to blame every broken window or minor property damage on the students. Blaming the students for everything became a running gag with Shadow. For example, if someone would say, "I've had a bad cold all week," Shadow would yell, "Goddamn students!"

"Drunk and disorderly" was not confined to the students, however. Sid and Shadow consumed more than their share of booze. When Sid had been drinking, he'd usually hit the front door around three in the morning, singing "Is It True What They Say about Sidney," to the tune of "Is It True What They Say about Dixie," and he'd head straight for the kitchen to fry himself an egg. This, of course, is where I slept and I usually had a few choice words for Sid on these occasions.

Sid, in fact, did have a serious drinking problem, but he was a good person and a hard worker. When there were no jobs available, he would help my mother around the house. He did a lot of the cooking. Sid sometimes worked as a short-order cook. By the time my mother moved the family to University Avenue, poor Sid had already seen more than his share of the rocky road of life. For reasons unknown to me, he had run away from home when he was a teenager, had been married briefly and had a son, Ralph Lewis, who was being raised by his grandmother on his mother's side on a farm near Morgantown. Ralph Lewis, who was just one year younger than me, visited often and, like the rest of the Knotts, he had a great sense of humor and loved joining in the fun at the dinner table. Sid eventually quit drinking entirely, remarried, and raised a lovely daughter named Sandy.

When Shadow had been drinking, he usually came home and went straight to bed. He didn't like any of us to see him inebriated. But one night, for some reason, he arrived at the front door, opened it, stood in the hall, and in a shrill voice he cried,

"And the little mouse crept in, crapped, and crept out." Then he went to bed.

Another night, Shadow apparently got into a scuffle in town and was put in jail for a few days on a drunk-and-disorderly charge. He was mortified. He tried to hide the news from my mother. He put the word out that he had left town for a few days, but he didn't fool Mom for long. When she found out what had happened, she packed him a box of sandwiches, cigars, and chewing tobacco. Shadow smoked cigars and he loved to chew tobacco.

She called me in, and said, "Donald, I want you to take this down to Earl, but I don't want you going into that jail. I want you to go around the back and get him to come to the window and you throw this up to him."

So I did as I was told, and when I got to the back of the jail, there was a fellow standing at the window looking through the bars. I called up to him, "Is Shadow Knotts in there?" He said, "I reckon," and he yelled for Shadow over his shoulder. I stood there waiting. Finally, I asked the fellow, "What are you in for?" He stared at me blankly for a second, and then he said, "Catching crabs out of season."

The fact is, all three of my brothers liked to drink, and when my brother Bill came home, the whiskey usually flowed pretty fast. When the three of them had a snootful, you could usually count on two things—singing and fighting. They'd start out by singing. They were pretty good. They sang in perfect harmony, and it was through them that I learned to sing a little tenor, which I made use of occasionally with Andy on *The Andy Griffith Show*. Unfortunately, quite often their harmony would become disharmony and an argument would flare up. Sometimes a fist or two would get thrown. I remember one night they brought a stranger home with them and a real free-for-all broke out. My mother was so upset she jumped right in the middle of the mess, swinging her broom in an effort to break it up.

These fights were never over anything serious, of course, and the mornings after were filled with regrets.

I suppose because of the example set by my brothers, and at the insistence of my mother, I rarely touched alcohol until I was past forty, but I'm afraid I, too, eventually began to overuse "old John Barleycorn," as Bing Crosby called it, and I finally gave it up entirely.

The Roomers

My youth was shaped not only by my family but also by the hundreds of roomers who came and went while I was growing up. When there weren't enough students around, my mother would rent to anyone who could put a dollar down—some honest and delightful, others not so honest or delightful. We once had a professional guitar player who graciously taught me how to play the ukelele. Not so graciously, he fled in the middle of the night, owing three months' rent. Others tried to lower their suitcases out the window and run out. The day before the rent was due, my mother watched carefully. But not always carefully enough.

Roomers came in all sizes, shapes, ages, and occupations. Con artists came and went. We had some real characters. There was a carnival barker and croupier who regaled us with stories of fleecing the customers. Then there was the absentminded college professor who inadvertently set our house on fire with his

pipe. That fire was put out easily. The fire in Tom Helfrik's room was another matter. One night after a quarrel, Tom's girlfriend got drunk, sneaked in, poured gasoline on his bed, and set fire to it. Fortunately, Tom wasn't in it at the time, but it almost did the rest of us in. My mother smelled the smoke in time to avoid disaster. Poor Tom apologized to my mother for weeks.

Mom's Religion

My father and mother had been active in the church back in the days of the farm. My father, I was told, spoke eloquently from the pulpit on occasion. My mother was deeply religious but she seldom talked about it. When the subject did come up, I was always surprised at the depth of her religious feeling. She simply did not wear her religion on her sleeve but was one of the truly good people of this world, more comfortable with the downtrodden than the high and mighty. She found time to help any soul who needed her. When Dad would allow it, she would frequently give up an entire day to take care of someone who was sick and couldn't afford help. My mother departed from the church, however, when it came to what was a sin and what was not. She was brought up as a born-again Christian. The fundamentalist church had labeled going to the movies, dancing, and playing cards as sins. Mom thought this was hogwash. As I've already said, she loved the movies and she was a passionate card player. She also loved a good story, even if it wasn't entirely clean.

Aunts and Uncles and Farms

Most of my aunts and uncles still lived on farms and most of them had the same religious background as my mother and father. During the summer, they would take turns bringing my mother and me out to their farms to spend Sunday with them. I hated those visits. For one thing, it meant attending a holy roller church service, which scared me half to death when I was little, and for another, it meant a long, lonely day out in the country. For some reason, being on a farm filled me with vague feelings of anxiety.

The farmers were nice people, but they didn't exactly set the world on fire with conversation. After church and a big Sunday dinner, the men would sit around with several minutes elapsing between sentences. I remember one Sunday we sat around for a full ten minutes after dinner before a word was spoken. My uncle finally said, "Anybody want to walk down to the gas station and get a bottle of pop?" I told Andy Griffith about this one day and it led to the writing of a piece where Barney says, "I think I'll go down to the gas station and get a bottle of pop, visit Thelma Lou, then home to watch a little TV," (long pause and repeat twice) driving Andy crazy.

In any case, those visits seemed interminable. I could not wait to get back to town. After my father died, my mother told me that one of my uncles had invited us to come live with his family on their farm. She wanted to know how I felt about it. Well, you can imagine my response to that one. She said, "That's good. I don't think I would care to do that either." I think Mom had become citified herself.

Haircuts on the House

Not quite all of my relatives were farmers, however. Two of my father's brothers, Uncle Lawrence and Uncle Frank, were barbers, and their shops were just a few doors apart, but they were different as night and day. Uncle Lawrence was a really devout born-again Christian who spoke frequently in the "unknown tongue," whereas Uncle Frank had long ago given up old-time religion. Uncle Frank was a fun-loving guy with a hearty laugh who enjoyed a drink now and then. He loved to play golf and paint. I saw a few of his paintings. They were pretty good. I saw more of Uncle Lawrence than Uncle Frank because Uncle Lawrence helped my mother out by cutting my hair for nothing. I spent a lot of time in Uncle Lawrence's barbershop, and I mean a *lot* of time. When I needed a haircut, Mom would tell me to go to his shop and wait quietly while he barbered his paying customers. Then, and then only, was I to take my place in the swivel chair. Sometimes I would have to wait all afternoon. Uncle Lawrence was pretty witty though, and he kept everybody laughing while he snipped away. I think it's safe to say that a sense of humor was pretty prevalent in my family tree. It was a different matter, though, when Uncle Lawrence came to our house for dinner. I would cringe when Mom asked him to say grace. You knew the minute you bowed your head and Uncle Lawrence launched into prayer that you were going to have your head bowed there for quite a while. For every time he started grace, he wound up speaking in tongues and time stood still.

A Lean and Hungry Look

Like Shadow, as a boy, I was painfully thin and had a general undernourished look. My family worried a great deal about my health. "Look at him," my brother Bill would say, "he can't even stand up straight." It is true that I caught every childhood disease that came along, and I nearly died of diphtheria. The county health nurse who visited our school was quite concerned about me. She came to see my mother and told her she wanted to enroll me in a special nutrition program at the university. The dieticians were planning to cook well-balanced, healthful meals for about a dozen needy, undernourished kids like me, hoping to build us up. Mom signed me up and every day for about two years I tramped over to the university for lunch. The food was quite good and I learned to eat some vegetables that I had not been able to endure. But to the dismay of the dieticians, I did not gain a solitary ounce.

The family was so convinced that I was in poor health I began to believe it myself. I was a budding hypochondriac. By the time I entered high school, though, I began to put illness behind me, and later on when I took my physical for the army, I learned that, apart from being underweight, I was absolutely physically fit. I'm sorry to say, however, that my hypochondria still shows up now and then.

Galusha's Grocery

The grocery store next door to our house was owned by the Galusha brothers, Harold and Sleepy. Their prices were a little steep for two reasons: you could run a tab there, and they delivered. My mother felt obliged to buy at least some of her groceries there because the Galusha brothers owned our house. She also needed the benefit of that tab more often than not. She bought staples there, like bread and milk, because their price was about the same everywhere. Mostly she trekked ten blocks to the A&P, a small store by today's standards, but the closest thing to a supermarket then, where there were bargains aplenty. She usually took me with her to help her carry the groceries. Now, surely the Galusha brothers knew we didn't survive on bread and milk alone, but my mother absolutely refused to walk past the front of their store carrying groceries from the A&P. When we got to within a block of Galusha's, we'd turn left and head down the street, through the back alley and around the other side of our house. No, sir, she just wasn't going to let them see us carrying groceries from the A&P and that was all there was to that! Fact was that Harold and Sleepy had the utmost respect for my mother, and I heard them speak highly of her many times.

Sleepy was a lot of fun, but he teased us kids unmercifully. Every once in a while he would grab me by my skinny bicep and holler, "Is your arm swelled up or is it always that big?"

My mother could make a whole meat loaf with just a smidgeon of meat, so once in a while I would march into the Galushas' grocery store and say, "Mom wants a quarter of a pound of hamburger," and Sleepy would yell, "Are you people having company again?"

15

My brother Sid, his wife, and their baby

They kept boxing gloves in the store and sometimes they would let us kids knock each other around in the back room. When I was little, they would occasionally take me with them in the truck to deliver groceries. I thought this was a real treat. All in all, my memories of Galusha's Grocery Store are fond ones.

Barney Fife and Other

The Neighborhood

My mother gave me a pretty wide berth to roam in when I was a kid, but sometimes I would wander even beyond the established boundaries. There were tons of kids in my neighborhood, but once in a while, two or three of us would head off into another neighborhood to challenge the kids to something or other. Or we'd head down past the railroad track to take a swim in the river, which was absolutely forbidden.

Influenced by the university, we were very sports conscious. We played a lot of basketball in the streets with hoops on telephone poles, and tackle football in vacant lots. It was certainly a marvelous thing to have a state university with a serious athletic program almost in your backyard. We were all caught up with the teams. We really looked forward to the football season.

I never paid to see a football game in my entire young life. Even if we had the money to pay to get in, which of course we didn't, I don't think any of the guys would ever have laid out the cash. It was too much fun to sneak in. Every Saturday morning there was a home game, we'd be outside the stadium circling the oval like wolves on the prowl, looking for a weak spot in the perimeter, an unguarded gate or an unplugged gap. We always managed to sneak in somehow, no matter what. We would even crawl in by way of drainage ditches when there was no other unguarded passage.

I remember one Saturday when four or five of us hadn't made it in by game time, we got quite resourceful. The football team dressed in the field house, which was separate from the stadium. As the team made its way across the street and into the stadium, they were accompanied by coaches and medics and water boys and so on, dressed in street clothes. Unnoticed, we joined in the rear flank and marched in with them. We sort of basked in the glory when a cheer for the team rose from the stands as we walked onto the field. We thought we were home free when suddenly we heard somebody shout, "Those kids, grab those goddamn kids!" Several guards came rushing toward us, and we ran hell-bent for the stands. Eluding the guards, we dove over the wall and into the seats as the crowd cheered our escape.

The Magician

My first acting performances were reenacting scenes from Laurel and Hardy or Abbott and Costello movies I had seen. I'd do these scenes for anyone who'd listen. Mom was my only real fan. She had infinite patience and encouraged me constantly. I have fond memories of marching around the kitchen, performing my head off while she'd be baking bread. She'd laugh in all the proper places and heap praise on me when I was finished. My mother's faith in me was immeasurably important in building my confidence. A reporter once asked how an underprivileged kid like myself way down in West Virginia ever thought he could grow up and become a movie star. "It was simple," I said. "My mother told me I could."

Magicians were popular in those days, and they frequently played Morgantown. Magic fascinated me and I decided at one point that becoming a magician would be a great way to break into show business. Every time I could get ten cents together, I would send away for a magic trick to Johnson Smith and Company. This midwestern mail-order house catered to kids like me by coming up with cheap versions of popular tricks. Everything was a dime, as I recall.

Each new trick that I ordered was practiced diligently. Then I would approach my brothers, who would be playing cards with some of our tenants. I'd try to break in casually by asking who was ahead. Sid would say, "Cabbage is a head, now beat it." "I'm here to perform magic," I would say with persistence. Shadow would crack, "How about doing that disappearing trick?" "Yeah, scram!" someone else would throw in. I waited until this ritual played itself out. Then I'd perform my trick for this inattentive audience. Rattled, I usually blew it. They'd call out, "Don't call us, we'll call you." Even when the trick did work, they gave me no encouragement. It was my first "tough audience." As I got a little older and began entertaining, I often wondered what Shadow thought of my talent and my chances of making it. I already knew what Bill thought. Bill always gave me love and support, but being a pragmatic businessman, he considered show business to be a high-risk gamble. He told my mother, "When Don stops thinking he's God's gift to the drama, he's going to amount to something." But when I finally made it, he was the proudest big brother you ever saw. I never knew what Sid thought, but he seemed delighted with the way things turned out. It was Shadow who really puzzled me. He seemed to go out of his way to downplay my talents. I finally mentioned it to my mother. "Oh, my goodness," she said, "He's very proud of you. He just doesn't want you to get too big for your britches." In any case, my mother was my best audience, and when I would perform my magic tricks for her, she'd whistle with amazement if the trick worked. If it didn't, she'd simply say, "Keep trying." And I did. To this day, I amuse myself and bore my friends with sleight of hand.

My brothers Sid, Bill, and me

The Ventriloquist

One day, Johnson Smith and Company ran an ad saying, "Send ten cents and get your ventrillo. Just put it in your mouth and throw your voice." I was in junior high school at the time and a fan of the most famous ventriloquist of all time, Edgar Bergen, and his equally famous Charlie McCarthy dummy. He was the rage on radio then. I never missed the Edgar Bergen Show. My ten cents was in the mail like a shot, but when the ventrillo arrived, it was nothing more than a bird caller. Even so, I'd struck gold. The little booklet that came in the bird caller package carefully explained the art of ventriloquism. "It is, of course, a matter of misdirection. You simply create the illusion that your voice is coming from some place other than yourself. Change your voice, keep your lips still, move the dummy's lips, and the audience's attention goes right to the dummy."

By sheerest coincidence, Harner's grocery, a few blocks down the street, was displaying in its window a real, if somewhat small, Charlie McCarthy dummy, complete with lips that moved. You could obtain this dummy with fifty cents and three Cocoa Malt box tops. I swilled Cocoa Malt like a chocoholic. Finally, with the box tops in hand, along with the four bits my mother somehow managed to dig up, I sallied forth in a driving rainstorm, under a large umbrella that my mother insisted I take along. I got back and stood proudly in the door, my dummy in one hand and my umbrella in the other. Shadow jumped up excitedly and came running toward me, hands outstretched toward the dummy. But when he got to me, instead of grabbing the dummy, he grabbed the umbrella, sat down, put the umbrella on his knee, and said, "Who was that lady I saw you out with last night?"

Doggedly, I practiced the illusion of ventriloquism, as outlined in the brief but helpful ventrillo book. Soon I could hold my lips still while the dummy talked. Growing confident, I decided to go to the front porch and test my skill on passersby. To my amazement, it worked. One woman even asked me, "Have you got a recording in that dummy?" Emboldened, I wrote a little routine, sprinkled heavily with jokes I'd heard Edgar Bergen do on the radio. Years later, we were doing a remote telecast of *The Steve Allen Show* from Havana, Cuba, and Edgar Bergen was a guest on the show. Mr. Bergen and I were chatting during a lull in rehearsals and I told him how I had once borrowed his material. He got a kick out of it. Then he asked me if I would hold Charlie while he went to the men's room and he handed me the famous dummy. My God, I thought to myself, I'm actually holding Charlie McCarthy in my hands.

One day, a neighbor asked me if I would bring my dummy and entertain at a little get-together he was having. I was a huge success. Not only was I a hit, they passed the hat and I came home with almost a dollar in change. I was in show business at last.

It wasn't long before I started getting calls to entertain at other parties and functions, and it soon became clear that I needed a larger and more professional ventriloquist dummy.

Bill Lough, a pal of mine who lived on our street, had an older cousin named Blake Herrod who was something of a wizard. A professor at the university, he was one of those multitalented men who seem to be able to do anything they put their minds to. He could sing, fence, paint, sculpt, and I don't know what-all. One day Bill told him I needed a new ventriloquist dummy and he offered to make me one. Well, he fashioned the most beautiful professional-looking dummy you could ever imagine. I was thrilled. *And* it was an original. No more Charlie McCarthy. I named him Danny. My mother made the clothes for him and Danny and I were on our way. I earned money performing my ventriloquist act at civic affairs, lunches, and banquets in and around Morgantown for the next several years.

My mother loved my act with Danny. Years later, even after *The Andy Griffith Show* and several motion pictures, when I would talk to my mother on the phone, periodically she would say, "Everybody wants to know why you don't do your ventriloquism anymore."

Danny and me

The Best Years

By the time I started high school, tensions had eased a great deal in our house. My father had died of pneumonia when I was in junior high school, and although my mother mourned him deeply, the burden of his many years of illness had been lifted from her shoulders, and as time passed, her spirits began to lift. I felt sad when he died, even though I had never really known my father, but I, too, felt a sense of relief. Things were looking up for my brothers. Jobs seemed to be opening up a little, and it began to look as if we might not be headed over that hill to the poorhouse after all.

My four high school years were the happiest and most fertile of my life (not counting *The Andy Griffith Show*). Whatever inhibitions and uncertainties I may have felt in my early youth, they melted away the day I walked through the front door of Morgantown High School. I began to experience a great sense of fun and an immense release of creative energy. I wrote a humorous column for the school newspaper, wrote sketches for shows, MC'd assembly programs, and appeared in high school plays. At the same time, I continued to do my ventriloquist act on and off campus. In short, I had a ball. I also formed a lot of new friendships, some I cherish to this day.

My New Friend

One night, I was invited to a roller skating party. Jimmy Davidson's folks owned the Davidson Funeral Parlor in town, and they drove a bunch of us to a roller rink in a nearby town, Point Marion, in the back of one of their hearses, which we got a kick out of just to start with. That night, I struck up a conversation with a boy named Jarvey Eldred, and almost from that night on, Jarvey and I became inseparable. We hung out together in school and on weekends we'd double date. Jarvey's mother would let him use their 1929 DeSoto, and we'd either go dancing or head to the roller rink in Point Marion. Jarvey was much smoother with the ladies than I was, and I paid close attention.

We also did shows together. Jarvey played the musical saw. He'd do "Ave Maria" on the saw, and I'd get a few laughs with Danny, and then we'd harmonize a couple of numbers and do a little soft-shoe. Later on, we added a third man to the group. His name was Richie Ferrara and he, too, became a lifelong friend. Richie had a beautiful singing voice and he played the mandolin. I'll tell you, we were hot stuff.

Cooper's Rock

Jarvey and I spent two or three weeks every summer at a cabin on a small lake in Pennsylvania owned by the father of our friends Tom and June Coombs. Jarvey and I imagined ourselves to be great adventurers and while at the lake one summer, we bragged to the Coombs boys that we would climb the treacherous Cooper's Rock Mountain some night.

On the night that we undertook this adventure, Jarvey told his mom he'd be staying overnight at my house and I told my mom I'd be staying at his house.

Cooper's Rock is a tourist attraction. The rock is perched atop Cheat Mountain and offers a breathtaking panoramic view. Cheat Mountain rises up from Cheat Lake. That night it was so dark with the moon mostly behind a substantial cloud cover that when we reached Cheat Lake, we had trouble finding Jarvey's boat. Eventually we located it and got on board to row and grope our way to the foot of the mountain. Cheat Lake is a treacherous waterway. It flows through the mountains and valleys in broad twists. The lake is deep, too. Trees poke up out of the depths

**My buddy Jarvis Eldred
with his musical saw**

because Cheat Lake had been valley. The lower end had been dammed up, and it is spring fed. Its real name is Lake Lynn. People said it got the name Cheat because it had a way of cheating swimmers out of their lives. We had never doubted that story.

The mission Jarvey and I undertook was simply foolhardy. It was the kind of thing you regret having agreed to, but are too proud to back away from. To scale Cheat Mountain in the daytime was risky enough.

As we arrived in the dark in the rowboat, the mountain slope seemed to rise even steeper than we had remembered it. Still, we tied the boat to a branch, scrambled ashore, and began our precarious climb. We were barely able to see our hands. We wormed our way up the slope, hugging the mountain face. The

Jarvis Eldred and me

higher we climbed, the dicier it got. Eventually we reached the point of no return, some five hundred feet above the lake. Each time we dislodged a rock, it would bounce once or twice, then after what seemed like an eternity, it hit the lake with a barely audible splash.

This was unlike Jarvey, but as we clung to the mountain after a scary slip, he said, "Maybe we ought to pray." That scared me as much as anything else.

The climb seemed like an eternity, but finally we reached Cooper's Rock, safe at last. Mercifully, our foolish ordeal was over. We said nothing but we both knew intuitively that we were no adventurers. We took the easy way down, away from the lake.

Back at home, our mothers had not been fooled. They got in touch and found out we weren't at the other's house. Jarvey was grounded for days. Mom let me off, the only advantage it seemed of being the baby. You were quickly forgiven.

Terrible News

During my last two years of high school, I worked part-time at the Warner Movie Theater ushering and taking tickets. I only made twenty-five cents an hour, but I got to see all the movies free. That seemed like quite a privilege to me. When I was ushering, I occasionally got into trouble for becoming engrossed in the movie while patrons were looking for seats. I enjoyed taking tickets too. Just being around a theater seemed like fun to me. I was happy with my job, happy with school, and life was good. But a dark shadow was about to fall.

One day while I was taking tickets, I saw my brother Sid walking into the lobby through the front door. As he came toward me I could tell he'd been drinking. He planted himself in front of me and stood a moment. His eyes were bloodshot and he was visibly upset. "What's wrong?" I asked. "You'd better change your clothes and come home with me," he said. "It's Shadow . . . Shadow's dead." I went numb. "Dead?" I gasped. "Yeah," he said. "He died last night at Bill's place. I don't know what happened." Shadow had been visiting our brother Bill in Illinois. It came out later that he had died during the night of an asthma attack. He was just thirty-one years old.

The next few days were shrouded in grief. My mother was almost inconsolable.

That first night after Shadow died, I was sent into town on some errand or other when a strange thing happened. Woodburn Hall is one of the most beautiful buildings on the campus of West Virginia University. It sits back about two hundred yards from the street and high in its tower a huge clock chimes out the time. When you walked from my house to the downtown section, you passed by Woodburn Hall.

That night, as I went by the old building, I looked up at the tower and was so startled I came to a sudden halt. The light in the old clock was out. I had walked by Woodburn Hall maybe a thousand nights and I had never seen the light out in that clock. How strange, I thought, how very strange that it should be out at this particular time. Then I remembered an afternoon a few weeks earlier when Shadow and I had been walking through the campus by Woodburn Hall and a man on a scaffold was washing the face of Woodburn's clock. Shadow had drawn laughs from passersby when he yelled up at the guy, "Hey, buddy, you wouldn't happen to have the time, would you?" It was then that I really began to miss him. It was a long time before my mother showed any sign of getting over Shadow's death, and she probably never really did.

The Big Apple

While I was in high school, my confidence as a performer grew through the encouragement of my fellow students, and I promised my close friends that after graduation I would head for New York and bring the Big Apple to its knees. One week after commencement, I was on my way.

My mother, as always, had been so good and so wise about the whole thing. She had said, "Remember, Donald, if things don't work out up there, it might be a good idea to come back home and go to college." A good friend of mine, Ray Gosovich, decided to join me in my little adventure. Ray wasn't interested in show business, and I was never quite sure just what his ambitions were that June morning when we set out for New York.

The plan was to hitchhike all the way, but after being stranded about two hundred miles out of Morgantown, we had to finish the journey on a Greyhound bus. This was not a good development considering the small amount of capital we had between us.

When we arrived in New York, we rented rooms at the William Sloan House YMCA on Thirty-fourth Street just a few blocks from the Empire State Building. We were in Manhattan, the year was 1942, and New York was still at its best. I was excited. That very first night I walked up to Times Square. I couldn't wait to see Broadway. Like so many others on their first visits to Manhattan, I was surprised to discover that most Broadway theaters are on the side streets and not on Broadway itself.

I was taking it all in when I came to a theater that was playing *Claudia*, starring Dorothy Maguire. This play had been a huge hit, but was now apparently coming to the end of its run.

Rehearsing a musical number

A sign in front of the theater indicated that the show was now on twofers—two tickets for the price of one. The idea, of course, was to fill the theater by offering theatergoers a bargain. I asked at the box office if I could buy just one ticket for half price. The rough-looking box office guy gave me a withering glance. When I didn't go away, he growled, "Okay." He sold me a single ticket for half the top balcony fare, and I saw my first Broadway show for just fifty-five cents. That balcony seat today would easily cost you *thirty-five dollars*.

I landed a job running an elevator at the Cornish Arms Hotel on Twenty-third Street, not too far from the Y. A lot of merchant marines stayed there. Ray did better than that. He was hired as a doorman at a fancy club on the Upper East Side. We took our meals at the YMCA or at one of the automats where you could get a fine dinner for fifty cents. We were enjoying ourselves, but we were also learning some painful lessons about the big city.

One day, I was sitting on a bench in the RCA Plaza when a fellow sat down next to me and engaged me in conversation. Pretty soon he was telling me how broke he was and how starved he was and how he needed bus fare to get back to his home in Pennsylvania. Before I knew what had happened, he had conned me out of five dollars. I only had *ten* dollars. I guess the hayseed in my hair was showing.

Later, Ray and I befriended a guy in the YMCA who was going to medical school in Boston. He had come to New York to see a girlfriend who lived in Greenwich Village, We hung out with him a good bit, and then one day he came to us with a telegram from his mother summoning him home to Boston. He asked us to lend him ten dollars for bus fare. "I'll wire it back to you as soon as I get home," he told us. That evening, Ray and I found a telegram in our mailbox. It said, "So long, suckers." Boy, were we angry. I never saw Ray so mad. We called that guy every name in the book. But the next day, he wired us the money. He had been putting us on and we fell for it hook, line, and sinker.

Years later I was playing in a golf tournament in Napa Valley when a doctor in the gallery introduced himself. "Remember me?" he asked. I didn't. Then he said, "Hey, Don, can you lend me another ten dollars? I've got to get back to Boston."

I, of course, had no idea whatsoever how to get connected in the show business world. Ray and I got to know some people at the Y, and through them I did get to do a show with Danny at the Y for which they paid me five dollars. This led to an appearance on talent night at a nightclub in the Village called The Village Nut Club. That was the extent of my chances to perform, but I did land a couple of auditions later on. In the meantime, I decided to learn as much as I could.

They gave away broadcast tickets at the Y, and I saw as much radio theater as I could possibly manage. I loved watching

Barney Fife and Other

the actors perform. I actually took notes. Whenever I had a dollar to spare for a balcony ticket, I would see a Broadway show. What a treat that was.

One day, I read that a bunch of stars were going to perform at a war bond rally on an outdoor stage in Central Park and I wandered over there to have a look. I enjoyed the show, but when Ray Bolger came on stage, I was completely captivated. Bolger was famous as the Scarecrow in the movie *The Wizard of Oz,* but other than that, I was not familiar with his work. He was a favorite of Broadway audiences, and that day I found out why. His comedy and eccentric dancing knocked me out. At the time, he was starring in a Broadway musical called *By Jupiter*. I went directly to the theater and bought a ticket. I became a lifelong fan of Bolger and followed everything he did. Some thirty years later, I had a nice chat with Bolger at a celebrity golf tournament in Santa Barbara, California, and I was amazed when he told me he had never taken a dance lesson in his life.

I finally landed an audition for the *Camel Caravan*, a popular radio program that showcased new talent. The lady who auditioned me was not very encouraging. After she turned me down, she said, "You seem like a nice, intelligent boy. Why don't you take your dummy and go home and go back to school." The words strongly echoed my mother's and I was beginning to lean in the direction of doing just that. The wind was clearly out of my sails, and I was beginning to get homesick. A few days later, with my tail between my legs, I boarded a bus for Morgantown. New York City was still standing upright, and I was the one who'd been brought to his knees. What's more, the humbling process still wasn't over. I spent the rest of the summer cleaning chickens in the stockroom of Raece's grocery store in order to pay my first semester's tuition at WVU. I was beginning to believe that brother Bill was right. I wasn't God's gift to the drama, after all.

Dressed in my finest

Barney Fife and Other

Back to School

I spent my first year of college working at the university employment office and studying very hard. A teaching career might just be in order. I didn't socialize much my freshman year, although I did become a member of a fraternity almost by accident. I knew I couldn't afford a fraternity, but I attended a few rush parties just for the hell of it.

Phi Sigma Kappa asked me to bring my dummy and entertain at one of their parties. I did so and afterward they invited me to pledge Phi Sig. I told them I couldn't afford a fraternity, so they held a meeting that night, and the next day they offered me a fraternity scholarship. I would not have to pay a penny to Phi Sigma Kappa for as long as I was in WVU. All I had to do in return was entertain at their parties and represent the fraternity at college talent shows and so on. I accepted gratefully and I did entertain at Phi Sig parties. Other than that, I made no effort to perform. Even Phi Sigma Kappa's affirmation of my talent did not raise my confidence back to the level it had been when I left high school.

All in all, my first year of college passed quietly and without incident. If it hadn't been for the war, I most probably would have become a teacher of dramatic arts.

Off to the Army

Few events in history were as unifying as the Japanese attack on Pearl Harbor, and most of us in our teens felt obliged to volunteer for the armed forces. With my freshman year behind me, at the age of nineteen, I went into the army. There had been quite a bit of amused speculation among my friends as to whether the army would even take me, and I was both proud and surprised when the army doctors declared me physically fit. The only thing was, I weighed in at one pound below the army's minimum weight requirement, and I had to sign a waiver. During the rigors of basic training, I must confess I had some second thoughts about signing that waiver. But by the time I finished basic training, I was shocked to learn that I had gained over ten pounds.

I trained with an antiaircraft artillery unit at Fort Bliss, Texas. Shortly after basic training, I got the surprise of my life. I received a telegram from the War Department ordering me to Fort Meade, Maryland, to join Detachment X, a Special Service unit.

Assembling at Fort Meade

When I arrived at Fort Meade, I learned that the army was forming a company to entertain troops overseas, and having listed myself as a ventriloquist on my entrance papers, I was chosen to become part of it. I couldn't have been happier.

The show we were to do was a revue called *Stars and Gripes,* written by a fairly well known writer in New York by the name of Harold Rome. But the revue was to be done only when there was a stage large enough to accommodate it. Otherwise, we would just do a sort of variety show with one act after another.

Talented guys from outfits all over the country began to arrive at Fort Meade to join the show. We wound up with thirty-five men in all; entertainers, actors, and musicians. We had a top-notch band and, in addition to several actors and comedians, we had three tap dancers, two singers, one magician, one novelty act, and, of course, one ventriloquist. The novelty act was performed by a fellow named Johnny Valenti. Johnny played the musical saw and the spoons, and he also got music out of a balloon and a tire pump.

One of the fellows in the troop was an actor named Al Checco. Al and I became good friends and have kept in touch ever since. Al is a fine actor and a good song-and-dance man. I was lucky to get to work with Al after the war. In fact, he did a part in *The Ghost and Mr. Chicken* and we also did a play together called *The Mind with the Dirty Man.*

Of particular interest to me were three highly polished professional comedians. Mickey Shaughnessy, for one, was to become a big name on the nightclub circuit, as well as a successful movie actor. Red Ford from Houston, Texas, was a seasoned and raucous comic, while Donald Red Blanchard, a hillbilly comedian from the WLS *Barn Dance* in Chicago, was one of the funniest and wittiest men I have ever known. Working on the same bill with these three pros was the best training I could have gotten anywhere.

Becoming a Second Banana

We began rehearsals at Fort Meade in midwinter. It was freezing. We were all getting to know one another, of course, and we plodded along slowly. Every once in a while, some of us would get on a bus and go to the USO canteen in nearby Washington, D.C. Now and then, one of our guys would get up and entertain the visiting servicemen. I did my ventriloquist act a couple of times, but I envied the comedians. It wasn't that I was growing tired of ventriloquism, it was just that deep down, I really wanted to be a comedian. Good fortune was with me because Red Ford, who was ten years older than I at thirty or so, thought that's exactly what I should be doing.

One night at the base, I was having a Coke with some of the guys and I looked up and noticed that Red, who was sitting at a nearby table, was staring at me and laughing. Finally, he walked over and said, "You know something? You're a funny little son of a bitch." A short time later at the USO, Red gave me a few jokes and coached me on how to play a deadpan comic. He gave me a cue when to walk on stage and interrupt him, and before I knew it, I was on stage playing Red Ford's second banana. We got huge laughs. We scored so well, in fact, that Red wrote me into his act.

The Send-off

After two months of rehearsal, we were ordered to perform the show for two Special Service generals. After the show, one of the generals gave us a pep talk. "Men," he said, "This is the first army show to go to the Pacific theater. As you know, *This Is the Army,* as well as other shows, have been widely heralded in the European theater of operations, but you will be breaking ground in the Pacific. We will be following your progress. Be assured that we will know where you are at every moment." We would soon be chuckling over those words.

A Voyage to Remember

We traveled across country by train to Pittsburgh, California, where we set sail for the southwest Pacific. We were to have a very long boat ride, some forty days at sea, zigzagging in case enemy submarines were on the prowl. We were on a troop ship called the *Seawitch* and during the voyage, Red Ford and I did our act for the guys. We got it hammered down pretty well.

In due course, we arrived at a port in New Guinea called Milne Bay. This was known to be one of the rainiest spots in the world, and it was raining as we dropped anchor in the harbor. We could see the steam rising from the jungle and the air was hot and humid. As we looked on from the harbor, the jungle looked beautiful but forbidding.

As soon as we docked, one hundred or so men were unloaded, but there were no orders for *us* in Milne Bay. Some of our guys had been getting into trouble for conning their way into merchant seamen's quarters where there was better chow and fresh-water showers. We had only saltwater for washing. The captain continually announced over the ship's loudspeaker, "Will the men of *Stars and Gripes* please stay out of the seamen's quarters!"

His announcement fell on deaf ears and finally he put our entire outfit on KP. But I'm afraid we wreaked havoc in the galley, dancing and singing and juggling the silverware. When the troops came by for their chow, each one of our guys did a little performance for them, causing the line to get backed up. General confusion ensued and the mess cook raised hell. The captain finally put our entire outfit on latrine duty.

Pretty soon the ship sailed up the coast to a port called Finchaven where the rest of the troops were unloaded, but there were still no orders for us. It seemed that nobody was even expecting us. We wondered if that general back at Fort Meade knew exactly where we were at this moment. *Back* down the coast we went, docking once again at Milne Bay. Word got to us that the ship's captain was beside himself. He wanted us off the ship in the worst way.

Our New Home—Milne Bay

We sat there for a couple of days and finally, I guess, the captain got through to someone because we were at long last ordered to leave the ship. It was good to be on land again. Notice I didn't say dry land. There was no such thing as dry land in Milne Bay, New Guinea. Certainly not at this time of year. This was the rainy season.

We were a motley crew as we sloshed through the mud and climbed into two waiting trucks, struggling with duffle bags and horns and props and carbine rifles and gas masks. I, of course, had an extra case for Danny to worry about. We were driven to a desolate-looking camp where we were dropped off at a structure laughingly called a barracks. It was actually no more than a long roof covering two rows of army cots. This was to be our home for a while.

I should mention here that we had been sent overseas without an officer. A sergeant had been put in charge of the outfit before we left Fort Meade and we were told that we would be assigned an officer once we arrived overseas. Several days went by while we listened to the incessant pouring of rain on the barracks roof before a second lieutenant finally showed up. He arranged a performance schedule through Special Services and before long, we were piling into trucks almost every night, heading out to do our show for the soldiers stationed in various areas throughout Milne Bay. The stages we performed on were, of course, outdoor stages. There were no seats for the audience. The soldiers had to bring boxes or whatever they could find to sit on. Because it rained most of the time, when you looked out at the audience from the stage, what you saw was a sea of raincoats

Danny and I perform for sailors in the Pacific

and helmet liners. If you wonder why they would sit on a box in the rain to watch a show, bear in mind that there was *nothing* to do in New Guinea, and I mean absolutely nothing. Most of the stages were covered by roofs, so thankfully we stayed dry when we performed. The stages were also equipped with motion picture screens and the men got to see a movie every now and then. Once in a great while, a USO show would come through.

Our show was beginning to click pretty well and the GIs were eating it up, rain or no rain. Donald Red Blanchard soon became our closing act. He was dynamite—with lines like: "I used to sing with my brother, but he's overseas now. He's in Wisconsin." Red Ford and Mickey Shaughnessy were tearing it up, and Johnny Valenti's novelty act was a sensation. Our singers and dancers were scoring, and something quite surprising had occurred in the musical department. For some strange reason, probably a snafu, the army had assigned four accordion players to *Stars and Gripes* at Fort Meade. Nobody had quite known what to do with four accordion players, but when we got to Milne Bay, the four guys formed an act. They were all Italian and they decided to call themselves the New Guinea Quartet. Man, did they play! They brought the audience to its feet every night.

The show was fun to do, but otherwise life in New Guinea was miserable. The constant rain was maddening and our clothes never seemed to get quite dry. Malaria was a constant threat, so we had to sleep under mosquito nets, and they fed us Adaprine tablets every day. Adaprine only wards off the symptoms of malaria and it turns your skin a yellowish hue. You could tell how long a man had been in New Guinea by how yellow his skin was.

Another thing that got old in a hurry was the fact that there were no walkways, only mud. Our poor tap dancers had no place to practice. One of the dancers, a fellow we called Silent Ben because he rarely spoke, solved this problem by building himself a small, boxlike platform. Wherever we went for the rest of the war, Silent Ben could be seen in front of his living quarters doing the time step on his makeshift platform. As you passed by, you'd say, "Howdy, Silent Ben," but old Ben would just grin and nod and keep right on dancing.

We usually wore leggings, but the mud still slipped into our shoes and slithered down our socks. Some guys grew a fungus on their feet the GIs called jungle rot. Of all things, I began to get it on my hands.

The skin on most of the natives was covered with large sores and scars and many of them had bloated bellies. We were told most of them had malaria and jungle rot and a host of other diseases. They were friendly people, but they spoke an unwritten language and communicating with them was difficult.

One of them, a young man who looked around thirty, began dropping by and visiting two or three of us. He had picked up a few words from the GIs and we managed to communicate with him. One day, I decided to try a little sleight of hand for him. I did my disappearing card trick and scared the poor fellow half to death. "Oooo!" he exclaimed, backing up with real fear in his eyes. I decided to show him how the trick worked just to put the poor man at ease. I demonstrated how the card just went to the back of my hand, but he continued to shake his head in disbelief. He wasted no time getting out of there that day.

On his last visit, the day we were to leave the area, we gave him a pair of GI shoes for a parting present. He grinned with delight, but when we insisted he put them on, his face grew troubled. These natives did not wear shoes, of course, and their feet were wide and flat. In an effort to please us, he stuffed his feet into those shoes and we laced them up. He bade us good-bye and walked very gingerly out of the clearing and into a wooded area. When he thought he was out of our view, he sat down abruptly and whipped those shoes off. It was sort of a mean prank, but we knew he would treasure those shoes.

Jack Benny Comes to New Guinea

After about three months, we left Milne Bay and headed up the coast to Finchaven, where we performed for another two and a half months or so. While we were there, Jack Benny came through with a USO show and we got a night off to see it. Before I took my place in the audience, I wandered around in back to see if I could catch a glimpse of Mr. Benny. Luck was with me because suddenly there he was, sitting all by himself in a jeep in the pouring rain. I guess he was waiting for somebody to take him backstage. The minute I saw him I started laughing. He had cracked me up so many times that the very sight of his countenance filled me with warm laughter. Every now and then I catch a stranger looking at me and laughing. I'm reminded of my reaction to Jack Benny that night, and I consider it the finest compliment I could receive.

I sat in the audience in the driving rain as Jack Benny walked out on stage. The GIs cheered for several minutes. They were thrilled to see him. To make sure you understand Jack Benny's opening line, I must explain to those who may not know who Dorothy Lamour was. Dorothy Lamour was a sex symbol who, dressed in a sarong, often appeared in movies that romanticized the South Sea Islands. Graced by the gorgeous Lamour, the Pacific Islands were depicted as the most beautiful and romantic places on earth. Well, Jack Benny stared out at the driving rain and the water-soaked GIs, as only Benny could stare, and finally he said, "The next time I see Dorothy Lamour, I'm gonna break her goddamn neck." Of course, the audience exploded.

A short time later, Benny came to see our show on his night

off. He was so impressed with Donald Red Blanchard that he came backstage and actually offered Red a contract to join his radio show after the war. I couldn't believe it when Red turned him down. But Red wanted to stay in Chicago and that's just what he did.

Red Ford Goes Home

One day, Red Ford became ill and wound up in the hospital. He never came back to the outfit. He was sent home where he finally recovered and, in fact, he came to visit me in New York after the war.

Mickey Shaughnessy, who liked the act Red and I did together, decided to put me in his act. Mickey and I were a successful team, and we worked together for the rest of the war, but I was always grateful to Red Ford for, in a sense, discovering me.

Another Famous Visitor

After a five-week leave in Brisbane, Australia, we arrived by ship at another New Guinea port called Hollandia. Hollandia was a little nicer area and it didn't rain quite as much there. I had had a lot of fun in Australia and I returned to New Guinea with a renewed spirit. One night after the show, another famous person came backstage, only this time he came back to see me. His name was Lanny Ross. Lanny was a popular singer when the war broke out. He and Rudy Vallee were peers. During the war, Lanny was put in Special Services as an officer. He told me he thought I had a lot of talent and invited me to look him up in New York City after the war. I told him I surely would, but I doubted that he would remember me. I was to be proven wrong.

A Look at the Navy

After Hollandia, we entertained in the Admiralty Islands located in the Dutch East Indies. The first island we went to was called Los Negros. It was a very beautiful white coral island, but we were nervous the first weeks we were there. Tokyo Rose, the American turncoat who broadcast to U.S. troops to sap our morale, kept saying in her broadcasts that the Japanese would soon invade Los Negros. We were still nervous in Biak, our next island. All we owned there was a slim beachhead. The Japanese held the rest of the island though they were cut off from their supplies.

Next we hit the island of Manos, also in the Admiralty group, where our navy, we heard, was preparing for an invasion in the Philippines. Vast navy armadas, literally hundreds of ships, were grouped around the harbor at Manos Island, and we entertained the sailors on several of these ships over the next few weeks. They fetched us in small boats. We boarded cruisers, battleships, and aircraft carriers. It was quite an experience.

Con Games

They fed us on onboard before the show and this was quite a treat because they usually served fresh food. There was no refrigeration on land in the islands, and fresh food was something we sorely missed.

One of our guys, a singer-songwriter named Dick Stuts, had a passion for ice cream. I mean, he loved the stuff, and with no refrigeration, of course we had no ice cream. But they had it on those ships, and when we took chow with the navy, old Dick would light into a con job. During dinner he would tell the naval officer in charge that one of our fellows, Bill Mares, just loved ice cream, and, well, this just happened to be Bill's birthday. "You don't suppose you could give Bill a great big dish of ice cream for dessert, do you?" How could anyone refuse a request like that? And, of course, how could they serve ice cream to Bill Mares without serving it to the rest of us . . . including old Dick Stuts? It worked like a charm every time, and Dick would sit there with this big grin on his face. The man had no shame.

The beaches in the Admiralties were beautiful, and swimming became our main recreation. Some of our guys combed the beaches for shells with which they made bracelets and necklaces. While we were on Manos, they sold these shell doodads to sailors when they came ashore. Boy, what a bunch of con artists we had in our outfit. One of them talked me into working as a shill for him. He set up a little stand displaying his bracelets, and after a few sailors had gathered, he started his pitch and pretty soon I said, "I'll take one." And I handed him five dollars and he handed me a bracelet. Sure enough, the sailors followed suit and bought every bracelet he had. I never did that again. I felt stupid and a little guilty, if you want to know the truth.

Good-bye Danny

Shaughnessy and I continued to do well and I wrote a short monologue, which they let me do from time to time, but they insisted I work with Danny most of the time. I begged them to drop the ventriloquist act. My plea fell on deaf ears, so when we sailed from Manos Island, I left Danny on the beach and reported him missing in action. From then on I worked strictly as a comic.

The Final Days

After the U.S. forces invaded the Philippine Islands, we were shipped to the Philippines. We did a lot of hospital entertaining for the soldiers who were wounded. We were on several of the Philippine Islands and we hit several ports on each one. We covered the island of Luzan from tip to tip.

At one point, as the war was nearing its end, the surviving prisoners of the infamous Bataan Death March were freed. General MacArthur gave us direct orders to fly to the hospital area where they were being evaluated and do our show for them. These men had been in prison for four years and had been tortured and half starved by the Japanese. They were still in shock. They filtered in to watch us, but they didn't laugh. They barely applauded. It was a sobering experience.

The war in Europe was over by then and the Pacific campaign was about to come to an abrupt end. When we received the puzzling news of the atom bomb and the war's end, we were in a province called Ilocos Norte on the northern tip of Luzan. Shortly thereafter, we were ordered to Manila to get transportation to the States.

While we were in Manila, the famous Danny Kaye arrived in town. He was to appear at the Rizal Memorial Stadium. The stadium still stood, a rare survivor of the war. We were camped nearby so we walked over to see the show. Like thousands of other GIs who filled the bleachers, I had never before seen this world-famous star in person. The place was abuzz until a Special Services general got up to say "just a few words." He got carried away, and the speech got pretty boring. All the GIs had been issued condoms, and they started blowing them up and throwing them in the air. Soon the air was filled with them; thousands of floating condoms. It was hysterical. The general droned on, trying not to notice, but finally he gave up, saying, "I guess I'd better bring Danny out here."

Return to College

It was Christmas Eve, 1945, when I stepped off the gangplank in San Francisco. I'd been overseas almost two years. It had been a tough twenty-two months, but I was keenly aware of how fortunate I had been to have served in the war as an entertainer.

I really think it's possible that I would never have gone into show business if I hadn't had *Stars and Gripes* to help me recover my nerve after that first bad trip to New York City. It seemed like Providence, working with professionals, going onstage with those comics and scoring with the GIs. Most of the guys who were discharged from the army were set back in their career plans. What's more, I came home unharmed. I was one of the lucky ones.

I arrived home in plenty of time to start back to college at the midyear semester.

Back to School Once More

I had planned to take a few months off when I got home, but I had experienced some unexpected anxieties and depressions overseas that still haunted me, and I decided it might be best to occupy my mind with some serious study while I readjusted to civilian life. It turned out to be a wise decision. I was on the GI Bill now, and I was able to help my mother out with a few dollars every month.

My life in college this time began to feel a lot like it had been in high school. Unlike that tail-between-my-legs first year at WVU, I began appearing in university plays, and, borrowing a few jokes from my pals in *Stars and Gripes,* I put together a stand-up comedy routine. I hooked up with Jarvey Eldred and Richie Ferrara again, and once more we hit the local circuit. Richie was very busy in medical school, but he managed to find the time for our bookings.

My confidence level was high, but I was about to receive what turned out to be a temporary jolt. Phi Sigma Kappa asked me to represent them in an interfraternity talent contest. The show took place in Reynolds Hall where all the plays were performed. The contest was being judged by a committee of professors. I did my new act and I thought it went exceedingly well.

I was quite confident that I would win.

Not only did I not win, I did not win second place, nor even third place. I went home that night in total dejection. Good Lord, I thought, if I can't at least place in a college talent contest, what chance do I have in the professional world? I spent a sleepless night. When I went to my Spanish class the following morning, my professor, Dr. Singer, asked me to speak with him outside. Dr. Singer had been one of the judges. "Listen," he said, "I just want you to know that we ruled you out last night because you are obviously a professional, and we didn't think it was fair for you to compete on an amateur level. Otherwise, of course, you would have walked away with it. I just thought I should tell you that." I told him I was very glad he told me. He would never know how glad.

Hitting the Pittsburgh Club Circuit

Morgantown is close to the Pennsylvania border and Pittsburgh is less than a hundred miles away. During our first summer break, I decided to try to get some club dates in Pittsburgh for my stand-up comedy act. I made the rounds of the agents, but I couldn't get anyone to book me. "I'm not familiar with your work," was their standard response.

I might never have made the Pittsburgh circuit if not for my friend Richie. "Listen," Richie said one day, "I'll go with you this time."

The first agent we talked to was a lady who'd turned me down once before. We chatted for a while and Richie began to turn on the charm. Richie was and is a lovable guy. Finally, he told her he was studying to be a doctor. "Oh, really?" she said, and she began to pour forth a stream of physical complaints. She was clearly concerned about her health. Richie began to give her some assurances and she seemed quite relieved. Finally Richie said, "Listen, what about my friend here? Don't you really think you could find a club date for him?" "Okay," she said, "I'll take a chance." And that did it. She started booking me and soon the other booking agents followed suit. Thanks to Richie, I spent the next couple of summers playing club dates all over Pennsylvania. I did club dates in towns like Meadville and Oil City, Wilkes-Barre and Cannonsburgh. They gave me bus fare, but I usually hitchhiked and pocketed the money. Hitchhiking, of course, was much safer then.

I did okay as a stand-up, but not what you would call great. I've never been quite comfortable on the stage by myself, and the only fresh material in my act was the one short monologue I'd written while I was in the army. Even that copied the style of a comedian I'd heard on the radio. I had not yet shown even the slightest sign of originality. But I was working and I was learning. One particular night I recall, I learned a little more than I had bargained for.

aracters I Have Known

The Dancers

I was booked as master of ceremonies for a show in a town fifty miles or so from Pittsburgh. I don't even remember the name of the town. This was a private club. When I arrived, I went around getting the names of the people who were going to appear in the show. I asked the first girl what she did and she said she was a dancer. I asked the second girl what she did and *she* was also a dancer. The third girl was also a dancer. I hadn't put it together yet, but what I was about to MC was a stag show. I had never done that before. In fact, I had never even seen a stag show.

One of the girls said to me, "Honey, as I take off my clothes, will you stand there where I can hand them to you?" All three girls were strippers and they stripped completely, totally naked. I stood there dumbfounded with my hands full of dainties. Well, I thought to myself, now I've done everything.

After the show, the piano player, an older guy, drove us all back to Pittsburgh. The three girls sat in the backseat and I sat up front with the piano player. It was after 2:00 A.M. and two of the girls immediately went to sleep. After a while, the third girl leaned over, and said, "Hey, Slim, where you stopping tonight?" The piano player yelled, "Now, you leave him alone. He's just a young boy."

I recall thinking as I closed the door to my empty hotel room sometime later, *I don't know why that piano player couldn't have minded his own business.*

An Important Decision

I wasn't quite sure what to do after I graduated from college. Should I head for New York again and go for broke? Or should I get a master's degree and have teaching to fall back on? In my senior year, I married a classmate, Kay Metz, and I decided to go to graduate school. I started at the University of Arizona, but had to leave before the end of the first semester because my GI Bill records got lost somehow and I wasn't receiving any money. I returned to Morgantown and WVU offered me an assistantship in tech theater.

During the Christmas holidays, I earned some extra money selling toys in a local department store. The fellow who was acting as Santa Claus was a big theater buff. He'd been to New York and seen all the plays. We'd sit and talk when things were quiet, and he kept telling me I should go straight to New York. "Go for it," he'd say. "You don't need any more college. You'll just get sidetracked." Years later, I'd tell people, "Because of this man, I went to New York and launched my career. Don't tell me there's no Santa Claus!" The fact is, I'm not really sure how much influence his urging had on me. I was certainly not looking forward to assisting in tech theater. First of all, I didn't know that much about it, and frankly, I wasn't really interested in the technical side of theater.

One day, before the semester began, I was sitting in the lounge of the drama department with some classmates when another fellow student swept in and cried with a flourish, "I have an announcement!" He was one of those overly dramatic characters you so often see in university drama departments. "Guess what?" he yelped. "Next month I'm leaving for New York." Well, when he said that, something snapped inside of me. *Dammit!* I said to myself, I'm *going to New York!* And just like that I made the decision. I rushed home to talk it over with my bride, Kay, and she was more than willing to go to New York.

I only had about twenty bucks to my name, so I hit up my brother Bill for a hundred-dollar loan, and Kay and I hitched a ride with some people driving to New York.

Lanny Ross Takes Me Under His Wing

After a dreadful night in a flea-bitten hotel on Times Square, our first night in Manhattan, we rented a small room at Ninety-ninth Street and Broadway. I still qualified for my service-related unemployment pay, known as the 52-20 Club, which meant you could collect twenty dollars a week from the federal government for up to fifty-two weeks. I took just two weeks of it. Kay got a job with the Celanese Corporation and I started looking around for odd jobs that would allow me to make the rounds of the theatrical agents.

After a few fruitless weeks, I decided to follow up on that invitation I'd gotten when I was overseas. You will remember that singer Lanny Ross came backstage to see me, and invited me to look him up after the war. Lanny was doing a radio show on the Mutual Network from WOR in New York. I thought it very unlikely that he would remember me, but I wrote him a letter anyway. Much to my huge surprise, I received an immediate reply inviting me to drop by his studio.

What a nice guy Lanny was. He introduced me around, tell-

Lanny Ross and me

ing all his people how talented he thought I was. Then he gave me a shot on his radio show. I did the monologue he had seen me do in the South Pacific. It was essentially a routine full of what are called malapropisms. I had copied the style of a well-known comedian by the name of Roy Atwell. Incidentally, I met Roy Atwell sometime later and told him I'd been doing his style of malapropisms, and he said, "Yes, I've heard. I don't mind. I'm retired. But you might mention my name." But as I recall, there was another malapropism comedian who preceded Atwell. He called himself Senator Fishface.

The routine I wrote is of a sportscaster calling a football game who gets excited and mixes up his words, like, "They're going back to their puddle. I mean, their *huddle!*" I still use the malapropism routine when I do personal appearances.

Lanny invited me to drop by the studio any time, and I made it a point to do so once or twice a week. One day Lanny said, "Don, do you own a suit?" I said, "Sure." (I owned exactly one, and it was shiny.) Lanny went on, "I want to take you to a luncheon on Park Avenue where Herbert Hoover's going to speak. Homer Croy, one of Will Rogers's writers will be there, and I want you to meet him." Lanny had taken me under his wing, and he introduced me to anyone he thought might be able to help me. Nothing came of my meeting with Homer Croy, but I was thrilled just to speak to him, and, of course, to hear Herbert Hoover speak.

Lanny called me one day and told me he had arranged a meeting for me with one of his agents at the William Morris office. I did my huddle-puddle routine for the agent, and he booked me on the Arthur Godfrey Talent Scouts program, which was simulcast on radio and television. That turned out to be a good shot and they paid me a whole hundred dollars. Next, the agent booked me on a local television show called *Kenny Del Mar's Schoolhouse*. One of the regulars on that show was an up-and-coming young comedian by the name of Buddy Hackett.

Barney Fife and Other

No Pictures, No Music

Vaudeville was being revived in New York, and the agents at William Morris decided to try me out in some of the vaudeville houses in Brooklyn and the Bronx. When I arrived at the theater for my first engagement in the Bronx, the theater's booking agent told me to leave my music with the pit band. I told him I had no music. "No play-on music, no play-off music?" he growled. "No, sir," I said. "They can just fake 'On Wisconsin' or some other college fight song." He gave me a worried look. "Well," he said, "Give me one of your eight-by-ten pictures to put out front." I gulped. "I, uh . . . I don't have any eight-by-ten pictures." "What!" he screamed, "you've got no pictures? Listen," he said, "you do ten minutes and get off, you hear me? Not one minute more!" Then he stormed off. Later I heard him telling someone, "The kid's got no pictures, he's got no music. What kind of an act is that?!"

I did the same act I'd done in Pittsburgh, and in spite of having no pictures and no music, I scored pretty well in these theaters. I told my agent I thought I was ready to showcase my act in Manhattan. They booked me into the Jefferson Theater on Fourteenth Street. This was the theater where all the booking agents came to look over the new acts.

Because of the laughs I'd gotten in the outlying theaters, I walked onstage at the Jefferson with all the confidence in the world, but after about two minutes, I realized I was in Trouble City. This was one tough audience. These people had seen it all, and I'm sure they knew the punch lines to every one of my jokes. Five minutes went by and I had not heard one laugh. I was beginning to break into a cold sweat. Finally, one guy in the balcony laughed, and I said, "Thanks, Dad!" And *that* got a laugh. It was my one and only laugh, and I walked off the stage in humiliation.

The next day I went to see my agent at the William Morris office. I was hoping he hadn't heard. He had. He looked up at me glumly. "I think you'd better get yourself some new stuff." That ended my brief association with William Morris *and* vaudeville. It wasn't just new stuff I needed. My suspicion was confirmed that stand-up comedy was not my strong suit.

An Unexpected Break

In the weeks that followed, I worked a day or so a week in a mail-order house. There was a fellow there who was supposed to instruct me on how to stuff envelopes. I wasn't very good at it. He reminded me of the guy back at WVU who swept in to say, "Guess what! I'm going to New York." I would be trying to get some rhythm into my work, but not succeeding, and he would come by, and calling me by my first name, which I don't care for, but he really liked, he'd say, "No, Jesse, no, no, no. Do it like this." And he'd smoothly slide the folded letters into the envelopes with a flourish, wrists flying like windshield wipers and never missing a beat, while I would watch in glum resignation. I'd wait until he left, then start again, moving as swiftly as possible, my appointed rounds to complete. I'll say this, it beat the hell out of plucking chickens in Raece's grocery.

In the meantime, I continued to make the rounds of the agents and casting directors. Every so often, I'd drop by Lanny's studio. In time, I got to know Peter Dixon, Lanny's writer, who had a long list of radio credits. Peter had a sort of twinkle in his eye, and he seemed to find me amusing. He surprised me one day by asking if I thought I could do the voice of an old-timer like, say, Gabby Hayes. I told him I thought I could. It seemed that Peter was putting together a western radio series about a twelve-year-old boy who owned a ranch in the Big Ben country of Texas. The boy's name was to be Bobby Benson, and the ranch was to be called the B-Bar-B. Bobby was surrounded by his foreman and protector, Tex; and ranch hands Harka; an Indian; Irish; and Windy Wales, the old-timer I was to play. Bobby Benson was slated for radio at 5:00 P.M. every Tuesday and Thursday over the Mutual Network. Pete didn't even audition me for the part. He hired me on blind faith.

That first Tuesday afternoon, I found myself at the microphone with a cast of veteran radio actors. Let me tell you, I was just about as nervous as a person could be and still function. Pete Dixon was in the control room, and when we went off the air, I sashayed by. He grinned at me. "Good," was all he said. I knew the final word had to come from the vice president upstairs. I went home fully expecting to get an official phone call advising me of my release. My body ached so much from tension that I thought I was coming down with the flu. These aches and pains were to become very familiar to me in live television.

The next day, a miracle! My telephone did not ring, and I was back at the microphone on Thursday afternoon, shaky from lack of sleep, but cautiously optimistic. *The Bobby Benson Show* became a big hit, and we went from two times a week to three times a week, and eventually to five times a week. It only paid scale, but at five times a week, I was bringing home a weekly paycheck of almost two hundred dollars, and that was pretty good money in the 1950s.

Our Playful Director

Having **been** a radio theater fan since I was a kid, I got a
real boot out of radio acting. There was quite a technique
to it, knowing how to fade yourself on and off mike, how to match
your voice to the action you were supposed to be engaged in, and
keeping your eye on the director as well as your script. The director directed the entire show from the control room behind the
glass partition, much like an orchestra conductor. Our sound ef-
fects man, our organist, who played our musical bridges on the
Hammond organ, our animal sound man (the man who did all
the horse whinnies and dog barks, etc.), all had to be woven in
with precise cues from the director. The whole thing fascinated
me. The show lasted over five years, and I never got tired of doing
it. On top of everything else, the *Bobby Benson* company was a
fun group of guys to work with.

Peter Dixon left the show after a while and moved to California. A writer by the name of Jim Shean took over the head-
writing chore. Our director's name was Bob Novak. Bob and Jim
Sheehan loved practical jokes. They kept teasing me about trying
to sound like Gabby Hayes. I didn't try to sound like Gabby
Hayes and they knew it, but they kept on about it anyway. Bob
would say, "One of these days, Gabby Hayes is going to come
after you." Then one day, I was standing at the microphone, rehearsing, when the studio door flew open and who should walk
in but Gabby Hayes himself. "Goddamn you!" he yelled, "you've
been doing me on the radio every day and I'm sick of it!" I could
have died. He kept on ranting and raving and I just stared at
him in agony. Then I guess he couldn't stand it any longer, because all of a sudden, he just busted out laughing. I looked in

Dressed as Windy Wales

the control room, and Bob and Jim were in hysterics. They, of course, had set up the whole thing. Anyway, it was nice to get to shake hands with Gabby Hayes. He was pretty famous in those days, but I must say, I didn't stop shaking all afternoon.

Bob Novak never passed up an opportunity to put somebody on. One day, just as we were starting rehearsal, Novak said, "Listen, Jimmy Boles just called and said he's gonna be about twenty minutes late. Let's have some fun with him." Jim was an actor who did the show frequently. Bob called the receptionist and told him to let us know when Jim was on his way in. He also gave him some further instructions. When Bob got the call that Jim was on his way, we turned off all the lights, and went dead silent. Momentarily, the door flew open, and Jim stood dumbfounded in the doorway. He rushed off to the receptionist, and in accordance with Bob's instructions, the receptionist told Jim, "Well, that's where I thought they were, but try Studio twenty-eight upstairs." In the meantime, we turned the lights back on and continued rehearsing. A few minutes later, the door flew open again, and an even more dumbfounded Jim hit the doorway. We continued rehearsing, trying not to pay any attention. Jim walked meekly in with a very puzzled look on his face and picked up a script. He took his place at the microphone and he never said a word about it. At Bob's insistence, we never mentioned it either. Many years later, Jim Boles wound up doing a part in my picture, *The Shakiest Gun in the West,* and I finally told him about it. He had a good laugh.

Cool Heads Prevail

Bobby Benson was played by a fine little actor by the name of Ivan Curry, but as the years went by, Ivan's voice began to change, and he had to be replaced by a boy named Clive Rice. Clive was a tiny little guy. He couldn't have been much over ten years old when he started. One afternoon, Clive gave us all quite an adventure. We were on the air, and we were just beginning the first scene of the show. It was a scene involving Bobby, Craig MacDonald as Irish, and my character, Windy Wales. Suddenly I heard a gasp from Clive. I looked up and saw blood pouring from Clive's nose. His face was panic-stricken. It seemed that little Clive had never had a nosebleed before, and it scared him half to death. He dropped his script and ran out of the studio. Craig and I looked at each other in sheer terror. I mean, we were on the air, and live! After stumbling around for a few seconds, Craig, while delivering Irish's line, held up his script and pointed to Bobby's next line, and gestured wildly to himself. He then paraphrased Bobby's line. Bobby's line was actually written, "I want you fellas to go into town with me today." As Irish, Craig said, "I heard Bobby say he wants us to go into town with him today." I gestured that I would paraphrase Bobby's next line. And so it went for the entire scene. We would do our own lines, then take turns paraphrasing Bobby's lines. This required reading ahead and keeping your mind on two things at once. I must say, we did a masterful job of it. The scene ended mercifully, and Bob Novak had the organist play a rather long music bridge. Finally, Clive was led in, complete with ice wrapped in a wet washrag on his nose. Pale and shaken, he managed to get through the rest of the show. When the half hour finally came to an end, Craig and I went limp. I didn't drink in those days, but as I remember it, I went out and had a drink anyway.

The Rodeo Circuit

The one thing I did not enjoy in the entire *Bobby Benson* operation began to take place in about our third year. The vice president in charge of programming, Herb Rice, who just happened to own the show, decided to cash in on the program's popularity by booking personal appearances. He called me into his office and made it fairly clear that I would be expected to participate in these appearances. Ivan, and later, Clive and I were the only ones from the cast who were sent out on these. An Indian fellow who had an archery act was hired to play Harka, and Tex Fletcher, who billed himself as the singing cowboy, played Tex the Foreman. Tex sang, Harka shot arrows at some balloons, I did a little "tall tale" comedy, and Bobby sang a song or two. It wasn't much of a show, but out we went. We didn't go out that often, thankfully, but it was just enough to be a thorn in my side. We played mostly state fairs and an occasional rodeo. We would appear at intermission in the rodeos. One night at a rodeo in St. Joe, Missouri, stands out in my mind. The four of us would stand in the center of the arena to perform these shows. When it came time for the archery act, the Indian fellow (his real name was Bob Douglas) would set up three balloons a good thirty yards or so away. Then with his bow and arrow he would proceed to break the balloons one at a time in quick succession. We would stand just behind him.

On this particular night, it was freezing in St. Joe and poor Bob, who was stripped to the waist in true Indian style, was shivering visibly from the cold. He was shaking so hard that he had difficulty getting the arrow in place. Finally he drew back and fired, and he missed those balloons by a country mile. He looked back at us, and then resolutely walked five paces closer to the balloons. We looked at each other, and then joined him. He fired again. A near hit, but no cigar! I couldn't believe it, but he started walking toward those balloons again, and we went with him. When he stopped, he couldn't have been more than seven or eight yards from the balloons. Hell, *I* could have hit them from there. He shot the three balloons and we got out of there as fast as we could.

Making the Rounds

Not only was radio acting fun, it didn't take a great deal of time. There was no makeup to apply, no wardrobe to change, and no lines to learn. For the *Bobby Benson* rehearsal, we showed up about three hours ahead of air time. We read the show through at the table for time, and made cuts or changes when necessary. We then rehearsed at the microphone with sound and music, then a dress rehearsal, and we were ready for air. This gave us plenty of time to pursue work on other shows.

I used this time to make the rounds of all the casting offices, making sure I checked in with each office once a week. It's interesting that you didn't have to have an agent to gain access to the casting directors in New York in those days. Television was in its infancy, and everything was up for grabs, catch as catch can. There wasn't a lot of money to be made in TV back then. The big bucks had not come into it yet. Some wonderful episodic dramas were beginning to emerge, like *Kraft Theater* and *Robert Montgomery Presents*. The leads on these shows were being played by people like Jack Lemmon and Paul Newman, who were yet to become major stars. Every once in a great while, I'd land a small part on one of these dramas, but I was frustrated trying to break into the comedy shows. Wonderful programs like *Your Show of Shows* with Sid Caesar and Imogene Coca and *The Jackie Gleason Show* were cropping up. Milton Berle, of course, had been there from the beginning.

I did everything I could think of to break through to the casting people on these shows, but to no avail. One day, in desperation, I called *The Jackie Gleason Show*. A man who sounded something like a gangster answered the phone. "Yeah?" he asked. Flustered, I said, "Well, uh, listen, who would I talk to about casting over there? I'd love to do your show. I'm a comedian." After a long pause, the voice came back, "We got a comedian," and he hung up.

The Birth of My Nervous Character

Most people don't believe me when I tell them the nervous character I did on *The Steve Allen Show* came to me in a dream, but it happens to be the truth. A number of things were swimming around in me, of course, that led up to the dream. Several months earlier, I had attended a luncheon during which one of the speakers was so nervous his hands were shaking visibly. He rattled the paper his notes were written on, and when he attempted a drink of water, he proceeded to spill it all over himself. It was a painful thing to watch, but at the same time, amusing. I wish I could say I suddenly thought to myself, "What a great idea for a comedic character!" But alas, consciously, it went right over my head. It was almost a year before it came to me, and even then it had to hit me over the head in a dream.

There was something else going on in my subconscious that found its way into that dream. I had been a big fan of the great humorist Robert Benchley, who appeared in movie shorts from time to time during the '30s and '40s. The shy, unassuming character that Benchley portrayed always struck me as so funny. My favorite Benchley monologue that embodied the uncomfortable, apologetic speaker was his classic "Treasurer's Report." I had been searching high and low for some kind of unusual character with which to hit the comedy shows, and I somehow managed to combine Benchley's apologetic speaker with the shaking, nervous speaker I had observed at the luncheon in a dream. I actually dreamed the first two or three minutes of a monologue in which the speaker, who is delivering an address at his civic club dinner on Ladies' Night, not only feels out of place, but is also so nervous he is shaking. When I awoke, I finished writing it. I was excited. I thought I had finally come up with a marketable, original comic character.

An actor friend of mine knew the owner of the Blue Angel, which was a chic nightclub in Manhattan, and he arranged an appointment for me to audition my new monologue.

On a cold, rainy afternoon, I performed the piece for the Blue Angel's proprietor, who sat at a table in the middle of his empty nightclub. To say that he was not amused would be putting it mildly. His reaction was so negative, in fact, that I put the monologue away, I thought, for good. It would be almost two years before I would bring it out and try it again.

Search for Tomorrow

The actor who played the part of our foreman, Tex, on *The Bobby Benson Show*, certainly took advantage of his time. His name was Charles Irving. Charles was a resourceful man who worked as a director as well as an actor. While he was still with *Bobby Benson*, he sold a soap opera to CBS-TV called *Search for Tomorrow*. This turned out to be a windfall for me. One day, Charlie, who had always been complimentary of my work, told

My friend Richie
Ferrara and I enjoy
New York in the early
1950's

me he had a running part on *Search for Tomorrow* he wanted
me to play. It fit into my schedule perfectly. Television soaps only
ran fifteen minutes in those days, in keeping with the time established in radio. *Search for Tomorrow* went on the air at
12:45 P.M. and rehearsal began at 8:00 A.M. There was no conflict
with *Bobby Benson*'s schedule there, so for the next four years, I
appeared from time to time on *Search for Tomorrow* in the role
of Wilbur Peterson. Wilbur was a neurotic who was afraid of
almost everyone on earth except his sister. She was the only one

Richie Ferrara and his banjo, today

in whose presence he would speak. As a consequence, I only had lines in scenes with my sister. The rest of the time I stared into space while the other actors talked at me or around me. This led to one particularly interesting afternoon. Bear in mind that we had to commit our lines to memory, and the show was on the air live.

I was in a scene with a fine actor by the name of Les Damon. I had a broom in my hand and I was sweeping the floor while Les was pacing back and forth, raving at me. Suddenly, Les stopped dead in his tracks and stared at me in desperation. He had gone blank on his lines. I, of course, could not help him because I was not allowed to speak. Les stood there for a minute and finally he looked off-camera and said calmly, "Line." The floor manager, after a moment of total disbelief, mumbled the line. I couldn't hear it and I knew Les couldn't. Les looked at the floor manager like he was going to kill him. Then, loudly, he said, "I can't hear you!" For a brief moment I thought we must be in rehearsal. Surely we weren't on the air. They had only one camera in place for the scene, but finally they brought another camera in to take a single shot on me while Les got his line. In all my years in television, I think that's the only time I've seen an actor actually ask for his line in a loud, clear voice, right on camera.

The part of my sister was played by one of the finest actresses of all time, Lee Grant. Lee eventually left the show and was replaced by another fine actress, Nita Talbot. The actress Charlie Irving hired to star in *Search for Tomorrow* was Mary Stewart. Mary stayed with the show for its entire run. Wilbur Peterson was the last serious role I ever played.

A Full Schedule

Shortly after Clive replaced Ivan as Bobby Benson, Herb Rice had some five-minute radio slots to fill, and he put together a little show featuring Bobby Benson, Windy, and Tex Fletcher, the singing cowboy. Tex and Bobby sang, and I told a tall tale. The show was written and directed by a talented young man named Jim McMenemy. This version of *The Bobby Benson Show* ran concurrently with the series. It was eventually increased to half an hour.

During our last season, Herb Rice wangled a slot on WOR-TV for the comedy-music version of *Bobby Benson*. This made for a busy schedule for me. On weeks that I was on *Search for Tomorrow,* my day went something like this: Arrive at the studio for *Search for Tomorrow* at 8:00 A.M., off the air at 1:00, then after lunch a rush to WOR Radio for *Bobby Benson*. As soon as *Bobby Benson* went off the air at 5:30, a mad dash to the television station for a 6:30 show, where Jim McMenemy would read me the tall tale I was to tell, while I was changing into my cowboy costume. I would more or less memorize it as he read it to me. I'd be off the air at 7:30, have dinner, then take the subway home to learn lines for the next day's *Search for Tomorrow*. After a few months of this dizzying schedule, I finally threw in the towel on *The Bobby Benson TV Show*. I would soon be sorry I did that. *The Bobby Benson Radio Show* was canceled, ending a five-year run. Wilbur Peterson was gradually being written out of *Search for Tomorrow,* and I wound up on the unemployment line. The timing couldn't have been worse. Our first child, Karen, had just been born.

Hanging by a Thread

I began knocking on every door I could think of, but nothing was happening. There's an actor's joke that goes, "I haven't had a part in five years. I wish I could figure a way to get out of this business." As the weeks wore on, I was finding that joke less and less amusing. Then one day, I read that a director named Perry Laferty was about to start a new television comedy series starring Hal March and Imogene Coca. I had done small parts for Perry three or four times on different shows, and he had indicated that he liked my work. I decided to call on Perry. When I told him of my plight, he said, "I've already cast my show, but I'll tell you what. I'll throw you a bit part or a walk-on whenever I can, because I'd like to see you stay in the business." Perry kept his word. Every other week or so, I showed up on Perry's show as a delivery boy or a hotel clerk or something. It wasn't much, but it kept me going.

Cromwell's Drugstore

If I hadn't run into Frank Behrens in Cromwell's Drugstore one afternoon, my career might never have turned around. I might never have met Andy Griffith, and if I hadn't, there would have been no deputy on *The Andy Griffith Show*. Not me, anyway.

Cromwell's was in the RCA Building, now the GE Building, in Rockefeller Center. The RCA Building housed the NBC studios and its many, many vice presidents. High atop the skyscraper is the famous ballroom, the Rainbow Room. Comedian Fred Allen once remarked that when NBC vice presidents died, they didn't go to heaven, they went to the Rainbow Room.

Cromwell's drugstore was an actor's hangout. I dropped in

there for a Coke every now and then after making rounds. It was fun to relax and touch base with your friends. I got to know Jonathan Winters in Cromwell's. Johnny was doing warmups for television audiences then. I thought he was the funniest human being I'd ever known.

On this particular day, my friend Frank Behrens was seated at a table and I joined him. Frank was a talented actor/comedian. He was a good friend of Tony Randall, and the three of us used to hang out together once in a while. Tony was a busy actor even then. I ordered a Coke, and Frank said, "Have you looked into that *No Time for Sergeants* thing?" I said, "What *No Time for Sergeants* thing?" "You haven't read about it?" he asked. "It's a new play. Maurice Evans is going to produce it on Broadway. They're looking for southern types. It ought to be right down your alley." (I still spoke with a trace of West Virginia accent. I probably still do.) "Here," he said. He pointed to an article about it in one of the trades. "I think this is the last day they're seeing people." I read the article. "You're right!" I cried. "They stop seeing people at five P.M. today, and Maurice Evans's office is clear down in Greenwich Village." I looked at my watch. It was 4:30. I flew out of there and dove into a subway.

An Interview with Destiny

It was exactly 5:00 P.M. when I arrived at Mr. Evans's office in the village. The man behind the reception desk said, "I'm sorry, but I'm afraid you're a little too late. Mr. Rogers isn't seeing any more people." Mr. Rogers was Emmet Rogers, Maurice Evans's associate producer and companion. "Please?" I begged. He looked doubtful, but he went into the office. He came back and looked at me forlornly. "I'm sorry," he said. I almost wept.

I was about to descend the stairs to the subway when I heard a voice calling after me. It was the receptionist. "You looked so sad," he said, "I went back and pleaded." As we walked back into the office, he told me his name was Van Williams. Van was also an actor and he wound up playing a small part in the play.

Emmet Rogers was seated behind his desk. He greeted me abruptly, and I had the feeling he was going to give me the bum's rush, so I started spitting out my credits as fast as I could, being careful to drawl as much as possible. I guess I sounded southern enough to audition, because he said, "All right, we're reading people Monday morning at the Alvin Theater. Be at the stage door at ten o'clock." On my way out, I asked Van if it was possible to get a peek at the script. Van said, "No, but it was adapted from a novel by Mac Hyman, and you can pick it up at almost any bookstore." I bought the book and read it that night. I thought it was hilarious. My God, I thought, Frank Behrens was right. It really is right down my alley. I could hardly wait till Monday morning.

Too Tall?

The Alvin Theater (now the Neil Simon Theater) is at Fifty-second Street and Broadway. I gave my name at the stage door and walked into a sea of actors milling around. Pretty soon they began to call out names, and one by one, actors took their place on stage and read with the stage manager. I was cold and nervous and there was no place to sit down. It seemed like an eternity before anyone acknowledged my presence. Finally I was given some dialogue to look over, and pretty soon my name was called. I walked on the stage and looked out into the empty theater. There were four or five men seated in about the fourth row, but I couldn't tell who they were. I was to read the part of Ben Whitledge, which was one of the leading roles. I had clued myself in to this character pretty well when I read the book, and I felt really prepared. The stage manager read the part of Will Stockdale, which was the leading role. When we finished, one of the men in the audience, who turned out to be Emmet Rogers, came running down the aisle. He seemed all excited. I could tell he liked my reading. He gave me a little direction and we read it again. He was more excited than before, but his excitement was soon tempered by a man with an English accent who joined him at the footlights. I thought this surely must be Mr. Evans. It was. "That was very good, Mr. Knotts," he said, "but I'm afraid you might be just a little too tall. Ben Whitledge should be quite short." Then he and Mr. Rogers walked back and joined the other two men for a brief discussion. Pretty soon, Mr. Rogers said, "Thank you, Mr. Knotts, we'd like you come back on Wednesday morning to read again, if you would."

I could hardly contain myself during the next two days, but

that you're-too-tall thing worried me. How could I be too tall? I was only five feet eight and a half. I only had one pair of good shoes, but I decided to rip the heels off. This should drop me down an inch or so. This turned out to be a mistake because when I stood on the stage to read on Wednesday morning, I kept feeling like I was falling over backward. It disconcerted me, and anyway, Mr. Evans repeated that he thought I was too tall. I was dismissed, and they told me I would hear from them in a week or two.

You want to hear about time standing still? I was learning that a big part of an actor's life is waiting for the phone to ring. When the phone finally did ring, it was good news and bad news. The bad news was that I didn't get the part of Ben Whitledge. Roddy McDowell was cast in the role, height notwithstanding. The good news was that I was offered one of the smaller roles. The bad news concerning the small role was that it only paid scale, which was only eighty-five dollars a week then. It was a Broadway show nevertheless, and I was excited.

Rehearsals

My heart was in my mouth on that chilly autumn morning in 1955, when I sat down with the cast around a long row of tables on the stage of the Alvin Theater to read aloud *No Time for Sergeants*. Maurice Evans opened the proceedings with a brief speech. He introduced our director, Morton DaCosta, and the playwright, Ira Levin. He then said, "My name is Maurice Evans, you may call me Mr. E. I will work you very hard and pay you very little." There was polite laughter. Then he said, "Let me introduce our star, Mr. Andy Griffith." I had never heard of Andy Griffith. He had a hit comedy record out called *What It Was Was Football*, but I had not yet heard it. There had also been a TV version of *No Time for Sergeants* starring Andy Griffith, but I had missed that too. In any case, Andy was still virtually unknown to the public.

As we read the play, I was as nervous as a cat, but I couldn't get over how good Andy Griffith was. When we finished, I was certain of two things: this play was going to be a hit, and a lot of people were going to know who Andy Griffith was.

The principal role of the long-suffering sergeant was played by Myron McCormick, who had been a big hit in the Broadway musical *South Pacific*. I was to find out soon that Myron had a bit of a drinking problem, but his work on stage was flawless, drunk or sober. There was one role for a black actor, and the understudy for this part was none other than Ossie Davis.

My small part was that of an army psychologist. I had one short but funny scene with Andy Griffith. In addition, I was asked to double as the preacher who introduces Andy at the top of the play. I was also assigned the task of understudying two other small parts.

The director, Morton DaCosta, known as Teke, wasted no time getting the play on its feet. We had only three weeks of rehearsal and three weeks of out-of-town tryouts. One week in New Haven, Connecticut, and two weeks in Boston.

During the first seven days of rehearsal, I suffered my usual insecurities. According to the Actors Equity contract, if the producers wanted to replace an actor, they had to do so before the end of the first week. After the first seven days of rehearsal, they could not let anyone go. I breathed a deep sigh of relief when that week came to an end.

I was a little baffled at Mr. DaCosta's direction. I'm afraid I had romanticized Broadway directors in my mind. I imagined that I would be made privy to all kinds of insight, and that I would receive keen direction. But the fact is, once Mr. DaCosta had blocked our positions on stage, he rarely spoke out loud, and when he did have something to say to an actor, which was seldom, he usually whispered in his ear. After fourteen full days of rehearsal, he had not said one single, solitary word to me. I guess I needed reassurance, so I finally got up my nerve and approached him. "Mr. DaCosta," I said. He whirled and looked at me as if he had never seen me before in his life. I was terribly nervous. "Well, I . . . er . . . uh . . . am I doing it all right?" I croaked. "Yes," he said simply, and that was the only conversation I ever had with the man. Teke DaCosta went on to direct two blockbuster musicals, *Auntie Mame* and *Music Man*, both on Broadway and in the movies. He clearly was doing something right.

I'll never forget my first conversation with Andy Griffith. One afternoon during a rehearsal break, I ambled out the stage door and found Andy leaning against the wall. "Can I ask you a question?" asked Andy. "Did you play the part of Windy Wales?" That took me by surprise. I said, "Yes, I did." "I thought so," he said, "I recognized your voice. That was a pretty good little show." We went on to talk about this and that, and I had an instant feeling that Andy and I were going to become good friends.

We Hit the Road

Rehearsals were over before I knew it, and we headed to New Haven. Audience reaction on our opening night in New Haven could not have been better. I was overjoyed with the way my little scene played. There was only one show that week that did not seem to play well. After the show, I ran into Andy, and for the first time, got an inkling of Andy's intense perfectionism. He began ruminating over the performance that night. I tried to be philosophical. "You can't win 'em all," I said. He looked at me intently, and said, "You can damn well try!"

We were a hit in Boston too. The show was already playing like a house afire. All except the final scene, that is. It was a scene that got almost the entire cast onstage for the climax, only there wasn't quite enough of a climax. We weren't going out on as big a finish as we should have, so every night after the show, Ira Levin and Teke DaCosta rewrote the scene, and every morning we had to show up and rehearse it. All I did in the scene was double as a guard, but I had to show up. They must have rewritten that scene a dozen times, and although they improved it a little, they never did get the strong finish I know they wanted. But the show was so powerful up to that point, and the audience had laughed so hard that it really didn't matter. It worked just fine.

The Thrill of a Lifetime

For an actor there can be nothing more exciting than an opening night on Broadway. When you're backstage before the show, you hear the buzz of the audience, all those first-nighters, those critics. Oh, Lord! You dare not even think about the critics! I had the very first line of the play. I had to go out there alone and introduce Will Stockdale, Andy Griffith's character. When the stage manager gave me the cue to make my entrance, I thought I was going to faint, but somehow, I managed to wobble out there and deliver my first speech. Then Andy made his entrance, and we were under way.

The audience loved the show. They laughed from the time the curtain went up until it went down on the final act. Yes, even the final scene. Andy was magnificent! He took curtain call after curtain call. Then we went to Sardi's restaurant on West Forty-fourth Street, where actors always went to await early editions of the New York papers with the reviews. When Andy walked into Sardi's, he was greeted with a standing ovation. The traditional wait in Sardi's was worth it. The reviews were superb. We weren't just a hit, we were a smash hit!

The First Season

It wasn't long before we settled into a comfortable run, and the play became just plain fun to do. The only fly in the ointment for me was the money. I had finally gotten my salary up to one hundred and ten dollars a week, but that still wouldn't quite pay the bills, so I had to hustle for TV work on the side. I would occasionally land a bit part that I could squeeze into my schedule. It wasn't just the money, however, I wanted to keep my hand in television. The play wasn't going to last forever. As a consequence, I was on the backstage pay phone quite a lot. Some of the actors would tease me. "Hey, why the hustle?" they would say. "Relax. You're in a hit." But looking ahead had already become my modus operandi. It's the only way to survive in show business.

The show usually went along without a hitch, but one Saturday night a little hitch did occur that cracked us all up, after the fact. Remember that almost the entire cast of twenty-seven actors was onstage in the final scene when the curtain came down. Well, on this particular Saturday night, the last line of dialogue was delivered, and we waited for the final curtain to come down, but the curtain did not come down. It seems that between the matinee and the evening performance that Saturday afternoon, the stage crew had had a few too many tall ones, and the curtain man had fallen fast asleep. Well, we waited and waited and waited for that curtain to come down. Finally, after what seemed like an eternity, we began to sort of straggle offstage in disarray. The poor audience didn't know what to think. There was a sort of sprinkle of scattered hand claps as we took our places for our bows. That one kept us laughing for weeks.

My worst personal hitch in the show occurred one night after about a year and a half. My mind wandered while I was onstage, and when I came to, I had no idea where I was in my dialogue. I hemmed and hawed and sputtered and sweated through the rest of the scene. There are loudspeakers in all the dressing rooms that play the onstage dialogue, so when I came offstage, I was greeted by the entire cast wanting to know what was wrong with me. That one scared me half to death.

As I mentioned earlier, in addition to the double roles I played in *No Time for Sergeants,* I understudied two other roles, one of which was that of Will Stockdale's pa. Pa was being played by a grand old actor named Floyd Buckley, who was in his eighties. One morning, I woke up with chills and fever and I thought I'd better call the stage manager and let him know that I was sick. "Well, you're a whole lot better off than Mr. Buckley," he said, "He died last night." So while they were getting someone for the part, I played Will Stockdale's father for about a week, with the flu and a lot of makeup. I didn't know much about makeup, and I had to get help from some of my fellow actors. It was one tough week!

Just as I had a hunch we would, Andy and I became good friends during the run. We had fun breaking each other up. We had common threads in our backgrounds, and we understood each other's humor.

Barney Fife and Other

A Gamble Pays Off

At the end of the first season, Andy left the show to do a picture for Elia Kazan called *A Face in the Crowd*. It was a good break and I was happy for him, but I missed him a great deal.

Andy had told me that he was also slated to do the movie version of *No Time for Sergeants* for Mervyn LeRoy at Warner Brothers. Several weeks later, Andy called and told me Mervyn LeRoy wanted to use me in the movie. I knew Mr. LeRoy had come to see the play several times, but I couldn't imagine that he wanted me to do my little part in the picture. I had a suspicion that Andy had talked LeRoy into it. About a week later, Warner Brothers called and wanted to know who my agent was. I didn't have an agent, so Roddy McDowell loaned me his agent, and she negotiated the deal. They needed me for just one week, and the agent (whose name I can't recall) got me a thousand dollars. Now, of course, I had to go to Maurice Evans and company and ask for a week off to do the picture. Evans said okay, they would let me out for the week, but only if I would sign a contract to do a bus-and-truck tour at the end of the Broadway run. As far as I was concerned, the bus-and-truck tour was out of the question, so I gambled. I gave them my two weeks' notice. When I told Roddy's agent I had turned in my notice, she was dumbfounded. "What's the matter with you?" she said. "You don't have another job." I wasn't sure what they'd do, so I sweated a good bit over that one. Finally Mr. Rogers called, and said, "All right, we'll let you out, but you have to sign a run-of-the-play contract." All that really did was guarantee them the rest of the season, so I said okay.

Only one other member of the cast was asked to do the movie: James Milholland, who played the psychiatrist. He was exceptionally funny. But poor Jim wound up doing the bus-and-truck tour.

Hooray for Hollywood

These were exciting times. Our son, Tom, was born just a few days before I left for the West Coast. Shooting my scene in that movie was one of the most exciting experiences in my career. Just being on the Warner Brothers lot was a thrill. It was a dream come true. Clark Gable was shooting a picture on the lot, and somebody told me I had just missed him. He usually took his meals in his trailer, but that day he had come to the commissary. He was known as "the king" then, and I was told that everybody stood up when he walked in. I didn't believe it, but years later, I was having lunch in the Universal commissary when John Wayne walked in, and such an awed hush fell over the room that I decided maybe they really had stood up for Clark Gable that day.

Andy and Mervyn LeRoy were already good friends, and they laughed and kidded around a lot. Andy's humor abounded, and he looked like he was having the time of his life. I know I was. Because of Andy, Mervyn LeRoy gave me the star treatment. He showed me around, introducing me to everybody, and even took me into the editing room where he was already working on the front part of the picture. It took all of about three hours to shoot my scene, and before I knew it I was on a plane headed back to New York.

Rebirth of the Nervous Man

I'm not exactly sure why it occurred to me to do this, but one night, after I got back, I decided to pull out my old nervous character routine and try it out on the guys in the cast backstage. While the apathetic owner of the Blue Angel didn't even grin, the *Sergeants* cast fell down laughing. This was more like it! I was thrilled. I decided to try to audition the piece again.

My first stop was Gary Moore's daytime television show. Now that I was in a Broadway play, doors seemed a little more open to me, and getting an audition with the Gary Moore people was no problem. The woman who auditioned me liked it, and made an appointment for me to do the piece for Gary himself. Gary loved it, and he put me on the show the very next day. He was excited about my nervous character and the routine. He took me aside and said, "Listen, we're going to introduce you as Harry Ommerly, one of our network vice presidents. It'll be hysterical!" Then he said, "I'm not going to let anybody in on the joke. Not even the cast. Let them think you're Harry Ommerly too." He clapped his hands with glee.

When I arrived backstage the following day, I was greeted with great respect. People kept introducing themselves and telling me how long they'd been with the network. When Gary introduced me, he went on and on about what a great vice president I was. When I walked onstage trembling, a worried hush fell over the audience. Then I launched into the routine, and they started to giggle, and soon they began to laugh out loud. My very first time with this character in front of a real audience was a huge success! They howled almost as loud as the guys in *No Time for Sergeants*. I knew now that I really did have something, and this character was an original!

The Tonight Show

My next stop was *The Tonight Show*. Steve Allen was the host of *The Tonight Show*, as well as the star of a very popular variety show on Sunday night. Much to my surprise, Bill Dana was holding the auditions for *The Tonight Show*. It so happened that I had met Bill when I was doing those bit parts on the Hal March and Imogene Coca show. Bill had been a regular on the show. He was now writing for Steve Allen, as well as auditioning talent for *The Tonight Show*. We chatted for a few minutes, and Bill said, "Let's see what you got." Bill was a great audience. He laughed throughout the whole thing, and when I was finished, he said, "When do you want to go on? Tonight?" I said, "How about tomorrow night? My suit's in the cleaners."

I was glad I was doing the nervous character when I stepped in front of *The Tonight Show* cameras the following night because I was truly nervous. I felt this was the real test. Much to my delight, once again, the audience roared with laughter from beginning to end. Nick Vanoff was Steve Allen's associate producer then, under Bill Harbach. Nick told me if I could come up with another routine they'd put me on the show again, so I went home and wrote another one. This time, my nervous character was promoting tranquilizers. I decided to repeat the circuit. I went back to *The Gary Moore Show* and did the new bit, and then *The Tonight Show* again. The new routine was a hit.

A Crack at the Big Time

Steve Allen was a very big star then and his variety show was very popular. Bill Dana said, "I'm trying to talk Steve into using you on the variety show." Since the variety show was on Sunday night, and *No Time for Sergeants* was dark on Sunday, I thought it would dovetail nicely, but I didn't allow myself to expect that such a good thing could happen. But a short time later, it did happen. Bill Dana called to tell me they were considering the possibility of trying me out on the Man-on-the-Street segment. This was a running sketch in which Steve would ask funny people their opinions on current topics in the news. Tom Poston and Louis Nye were already appearing in the spot. I had seen the show a few times, and Tom and Louie had broken me up. Louie was the campy, dapper sophisticate, who made the phrase "Hi-ho, Steverino" famous, and Tom Poston was the goofy guy who couldn't remember his own name. Steve Allen would ask, "And what is your name, sir?" Tom would then roll his eyes up in his head, thinking as hard as he could until Steve would finally say, "Never mind, we'd better go on."

One Sunday, Tom Poston had to go out of town. They needed

Steve Allen, Louis Nye, and me

Barney Fife and Other

someone to fill in and called me to do my nervous character in the Man on the Street. Steve Allen had a crack writing staff: Herb Sargent, Stan Burns, Bill Dana, Don Hinkley, Arnie Sultan, and Marvin Worth, headed up by Leonard Stern. They wrote a very funny bit for me. When the camera came up on me, I was shaking like a leaf. Steve Allen asked, "Are you nervous?" "Nope!" I shot back, bugging my eyes, and the house came down. The laugh was so big and so sudden, in fact, that it startled me. The rest of the bit played beautifully, and I was asked to come back the following week. This time with Louie *and* Tom. They asked me back every week, as it turned out, for the remainder of the season.

A New Career

Between *No Time for Sergeants* and *The Steve Allen Show*, I was now working seven days a week and, once again, I was growing weary from overwork. I asked Emmet Rogers to let me out of the play. *Sergeants* was nearing the end of its second season and its close, and I knew they had already set someone to play my role in the tour, so they had an actor ready to step in. Even so, they gave me a hard time for a couple of weeks, but they finally gave me my release.

Up to this point, I had been working *The Steve Allen Show* without a contract. I was doing one show at a time with no guarantee, but toward the end of the season, they finally offered me a three-year contract.

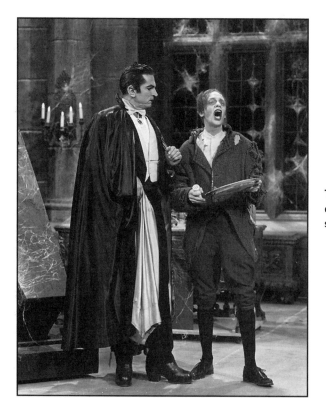

Tom Poston and me dressed for a Dracula sketch

The Man on the Street

om Poston and Louis Nye are gifted comedians, and they
were so delightful to work with. Each of us was under pressure to get our laughs every week, and I think the common challenge drew us together. Even though we were, in a sense, competing, we pulled for one another and there was a feeling of comraderie. In any case, despite the pressures, we had great fun and enjoyed each other's humor. Tom and I stayed pretty close to script, but Louie was given to improvising and would frequently come up with an ad lib from left field that would knock

The whole *Allen* cast around the piano

you right off your feet. Louie's ad libs usually broke Steve Allen up, which always delighted the audience.

The popularity of the Man on the Street was growing in leaps and bounds, and fame was becoming a part of our lives. I must say I had difficulty adjusting to this phenomenon. People began pointing me out on the street and asking me for my autograph, and I was constantly asked, "Are you nervous?" I felt obliged to throw them my "Nope" answer, but I was growing tired of the question. I wondered if they thought I really was that nervous. The fact is, this instant fame *was* quite nerve-wracking. I became very self-conscious and began to avoid public places whenever possible. I was learning that fame exacted a price. On the one hand, receiving recognition was gratifying, but on the other, losing one's anonymity was uncomfortable, in fact, sometimes downright painful. It would be several years before I would be at ease with celebrity fame. And yet, ambition drove me harder and harder to become as good and as funny as possible each and every week. The writers usually wrote wonderful stuff for us, but if they didn't, I would lie awake at night, trying to come up with something better.

In the Man-on-the-Street sketches, my name was always Morrison, with two initials preceding, which would get a laugh when tied into the profession I told Steve I was in. For example, one week, Steve asked, "What is your name, sir?" Shaking like a leaf, I said, "My name is S. L. Morrison and I'm a plastic surgeon." Steve then asked, "What does S. L. stand for?" "Sorry, lady!" I shot back. We would then do two or three more jokes usually based on my nervousness. I think the funniest one that I came up with from lying awake at night went like this:

STEVE: Your name, sir?
DON *(shaking)*: My name is K. B. Morrison, and I used to work in a munitions factory.
STEVE: What does the K. B. stand for?
DON: Kaboom!
STEVE: You say you *used* to work in a munitions factor. You don't work there anymore?
DON: It isn't there anymore.

Barney Fife and Other

Tom Poston

Guest Stars

I n addition to the Man-on-the-Street segments, Steve used Tom and Louis and me as supporting comics in other sketches, and occasionally gave each of us the lead in a sketch.

The Steve Allen Show was not only popular, it was considered to be hip by show people, and Steve had no problem booking the biggest stars in the business as guests on the show. Stars like Orson Welles, Mickey Rooney, Jack Lemmon, Henry Fonda, Louis Armstrong, Tony Bennett, Lena Horne, yes, and even Elvis

Presley, just to name a few, graced our stage. One guest star who showed up a couple of times was . . . guess who? Andy Griffith.

It was a real kick working with these people, most of whom I had admired from afar. Sometimes I would be so awed by their presence that I would become truly nervous. On one show, during a swing dance scene, I had to dance with Claudette Colbert. I became so unglued I stepped on her feet at least half a dozen times. She did not appreciate it! I could have died. Lou Costello did the show several times, and Tom and Louie and I got to take turns doing Abbott's part in some of the old Abbott and Costello sketches. Now, that was a real kick. Bud Abbott had retired, and Lou really enjoyed working with us on the show. He was a wonderfully sweet man.

The legendary Errol Flynn did a guest shot with us. The poor man was not well by this time, and he was just a little drunk during the entire week of rehearsal, but he did the show just fine. He had a wonderful sense of humor. We did a takeoff on *To Tell the Truth*. When Steve said, "Will the real Errol Flynn stand up, and I stood up, Errol Flynn almost fell off his chair laughing. But it was sad to see this Hollywood legend on the bottom rung of the ladder. As we left the theater after the show that night, we found him sitting on the dressing room stairs with his head in his hands. He died a short time after that.

Barney Fife and Other

Top People

Steve Allen surrounded himself with good people behind the camera, as well as in front. The show was produced by a lovable fellow named Bill Harbach, and a keen-witted man named Nick Vanoff. They ran the show pleasantly and efficiently. As you can imagine, a live variety show with rotating guest stars and a constant consumption of new comedy material is not an easy operation to organize.

Our cameraman was a perfectionist named Dwight Hemion. Dwight was one of the best. He insisted on good pictures, and when we had a gorgeous guest star like Lena Horne, he would spend hours lining up shots on her numbers. This would make for a long camera rehearsal on show day. We went on the air at 8:00 on Sunday night, and we often had to be at the theater at 7:00 A.M.

Steve was always on the lookout for new talent, and by the time we reached the end of our third season, he had added four new supporting comics to the cast: Pat Harrington, Jr., Dayton Allen, Gabe Dell, and Bill Dana. Bill Dana had developed his famous José Jiménez character, who was added to the Man on the Street. Bill continued writing for the show as well. All four of these fellows were delightful comics and they brought new blood into the show. But, of course, it cut down on the camera time that Tom and Louie and I had previously enjoyed. Much to our credit, however, I don't think we ever bore any serious resentment. They were truly funny guys, and they added to the show. As a matter of fact, in retrospect, I think it was quite remarkable that in a show with so many talented, ambitious people, there were never any visible signs of temperament or professional jealousy.

Leonard Stern

Beside serving as our head writer, Leonard Stern directed the sketches, and he was a taskmaster. Lenny had a tremendous knowledge of comedy and a good sense of what would work and what would not. He came to the show with a long list of credits, not the least of which was writing for the great Jackie Gleason. Jackie had brought Leonard from the West Coast to New York to write for the famous *Honeymooners* which starred Jackie, Art Carney, and Audrey Meadows. In those days, when Jackie Gleason got too heavy, he would check into Doctors Hospital to diet. When Leonard arrived in New York, he went to the hospital to say hello to Jackie. "I'm sorry," the nurse told him. "Mr. Gleason wasn't feeling well and he went home."

Leonard was exacting and could be tough to work for, but he was great at inspiring us with confidence in our material. We were out there live and there were no laugh tracks. If the audience didn't laugh, you died, period! Having confidence in your material was half the battle. Leonard's importance to us in that regard came home to us one Sunday in particular. Because of a family emergency, Lenny was not able to be with us during the entire week of rehearsal. It so happened that we had a sketch that very week that seemed to us to be weak. We walked gravely through it all week, and by the time Sunday rolled around, we were convinced it really stank. Lenny arrived on show day to find us down in the mouth. "Are you kidding?" he screamed. "That is a funny sketch!" He began pacing back and forth, extolling the virtues of the sketch. He would recite a line and shout, "That's not funny?" It was a regular halftime pep talk. We went out and sold the sketch. It wasn't the funniest material in the world, but we made it work, and that was a lesson I have never forgotten. Leonard Stern went on to create and produce many successful television shows, including *Get Smart,* starring Don Adams.

No Prompter, Thank You

I think my most terrifying experience in live television occurred on *The Steve Allen Show.* I wrote a monologue about a political candidate speaking to his workers, and Lenny Stern scheduled me to perform it on the show. The day before the show, the floor manager asked me for a copy of the piece in order to put it on the TelePrompTer. The TelePrompTer is a sort of moving scroll that contains the dialogue of the show, which the actors can read or refer to if they need it. Most variety shows use TelePrompTers or cue cards, whereas most dramatic shows do not. I told the floor manager, "I don't think you need to put my monologue on prompter. I wrote it and it's pretty well burned into my memory." Oh, how I lived to regret those words.

On the night of the show, I started the monologue and was sailing along pretty well, getting some good laughs, when all of a sudden, for some reason, I froze up. My mind went totally blank. I had no idea what my next line was. I looked around helplessly. The TelePrompTers were dark and still. I was all alone out there and there was no help to be gotten from anything or anyone. I was enveloped in sheer terror. I considered simply walking off the stage, but thought better of it, and began fumphing around, ad-libbing nonsense. Finally, after what seemed an

Louis Nye, Tom Poston, and me dressed in our finest

eternity but was probably only around fifteen or twenty seconds, my next line jumped into my head. Gratefully, I finished the piece and when I was safe backstage, I fell into a dead heap. What a terrifying experience! The amazing thing about it, though, was that after talking to people who'd been in the audience, I learned that no one even noticed that I had had a problem. Amazing!

My Cuban Crisis

Shortly before the Castro revolution in Cuba, Steve Allen got permission from NBC to do a remote broadcast of our show from Havana. I felt like I was coming down with a flu bug when we flew out of New York, and I was looking forward to the warm climate in Cuba, but unfortunately, Cuba was being hit by a rare winter cold spell. The Cubans were freezing their tails off, and I was going from bad to worse.

I mentioned earlier that Edgar Bergen was one of our guest stars that week, and Lou Costello was the other. It so happened that Abbott and Costello movies were being played heavily on Cuban television at the time, and the Cubans were treating Lou like a hot celebrity. They were all over him for his autograph. Lou got a big kick out of it.

In any case, I enjoyed rehearsing with Bergen and Costello, but by the second day, I was feeling really sick. My temperature started to climb, so I asked the hotel to send a doctor up to see me. We were staying at the Havana Riviera. The Cuban doctor did not speak much English, and even though I had taken Spanish in college, I was not able to understand a word he said. My hypochondria took over and I began to worry that I wasn't going to be able to make the show.

My friend Richie Ferrara had become a doctor and was practicing in Gross Pointe, Michigan. I picked up the phone and called Richie. "Listen," I said, "I'm sick as hell down here and even though I should, I don't understand Spanish, and I have no idea what these doctors are telling me. Will you be a pal and fly down here and give me a hand?" Much to my surprise and delight, Richie said, "I'll be there tomorrow." Richie arrived the next morning and when he saw how distraught I was, he gave me a very strong tranquilizer. After a while, he said, "I want you to come downstairs with me to the coffee shop. I think you should try to eat something."

When we were seated in the coffee shop, I ordered some tea and sweetened it with sugar. I took a big swig of sweet tea and the next thing I knew, I was lying flat on my back, looking up at Richie and a bunch of people hovering over me, rubbing my wrists and fanning me. For the only time in my entire life, I had fainted. Apparently, the strong tranquilizer had lowered my blood pressure, and the swallow of hot tea had done the rest.

Richie prescribed some other good stuff, and under his care, I did make the show. I also made *Time* magazine. They wrote, "Don Knotts fainted from nervous exhaustion in the coffee shop of the Havana Riviera hotel." They always had to put that word "nervous" in there. Richie and I still laugh over this incident.

The *Steve Allen* cast reunited in 1975

Sherwin Bash

I t was during *The Steve Allen Show* that I decided I needed representation. I signed with a young personal manager by the name of Sherwin Bash, who was managing Louie Nye at the time. Sherwin had two partners: Mace Neufeld and Alan Bernard. They called themselves BNB Associates. Alan Bernard left the firm early on. Sherwin and Mace remained partners for over thirty years. In recent years, Mace Neufeld quit managing to become a successful motion picture producer. Sherwin and I have been through thick and thin these forty years together, and he's a good friend, as well as a manager. Sherwin is extremely knowledgeable about our business and I've leaned heavily on his counsel.

Abby the Agent

In 1959, Steve Allen asked NBC to move the show to the West Coast. When I learned that we were moving to Los Angeles, I realized it was time to find an agent. My friend Tony Randall recommended his own agent, Abby Greshler. Abby was a very successful agent on the West Coast. When Dean Martin and Jerry Lewis were a comedy team at their height, Abby had been their agent. Besides Tony Randall, Abby represented David Janssen and Vince Edwards. David was the star of the television series *The Fugitive,* and Vince Edwards starred in *Ben Casey.*

Abby Greshler was a legend in Hollywood. He was the last of the old-time agents. He was brash, pushy, and cunning, and yet he could be oh so lovable! Producers would close their eyes and shake their heads at the very mention of his name. Abby was thin and emaciated and his skin had a sort of sour green hue to it. He was often described as looking like a corpse, but you dared not let that fool you. He was as healthy as a horse, and he never ran out of energy when he was chasing after a deal.

Abby went to great lengths to keep himself conspicuous. He used to take his clients to lunch at the fashionable La Scala restaurant in Beverly Hills. There were no cell phones in those days, of course, but that was no problem for Abby. He never failed to be paged to the phone the minute he arrived at La Scala. He would then shout, "Waiter, would you bring a phone to my table, please!" Everybody knew these calls were orchestrated by Abby.

One of my first personal experiences with Abby came shortly after I'd moved to Los Angeles. He wanted me to meet the casting director at MGM, and he picked me up in his car. As we approached the front gate, which was open, instead of slowing down, Abby began to pick up speed, and we drove through the gate without stopping. As we went through, the guard yelled, "Abby Greshler, you're barred from this lot!" Abby gave him the finger. When we got to the casting director's office (I can't remember his name), we approached his secretary, who told us he was in a meeting. Abby said, "That's all right, we'll wait." She said, "No, no, he'll be busy for the next couple of hours." "We'll wait," Abby insisted. We sat down and by and by, the secretary left the room. Abby grabbed my arm. "Come on!" He opened the door to the casting director's private office, and pushed me through. Four men were seated around the desk. They looked at us in disbelief. Abby went over and shook hands with everybody. "Just wanted you to say hello to Don Knotts," he said, "funniest guy on *The Steve Allen Show*. Keep him in mind." And out we went. Did that take chutzpah or what?

I think one of the most outrageous things I ever saw Abby do happened on one of Lena Horne's opening nights at the Coconut Grove. The audience was made up largely of invited guests, most of whom were people in the business. Abby had wangled a table for eight and had invited Vince Edwards, David Janssen, myself, and our wives. I think Tony Randall was in New York at the time. It was a gala evening. The dress was formal and the place was filled with stars. When we arrived, we took our place in a short line of people who were cued up to be seated. While we were standing there, Abby Greshler came in. Ignoring the line, he walked straight to the maître d'. Talking a mile a minute, he began pressing himself against the maître d', who began to back up. Groans of protest rose from the line. I heard someone say, "Don't let that son of a bitch in!" But sure enough, no sooner had that been said than Abby disappeared into the show room. The line booed.

When they showed us to our table, Abby was arguing with

the headwaiter. He was dissatisfied with the table. He had been assured, he said, that he would be given a ringside table. The table he had been offered was one row back. We all stood there while Abby yelled, "Goddammit! I brought Martin and Lewis in here and put this place on the map, and you people treat me like this? I want to see the top man!" "Yes, sir, follow me," said the waiter. As Abby left, he shouted to us, "Don't sit down at that table!" The five of us stood there awkwardly for a moment. Finally, Abby's wife, Vi, said, "I think we'd better go ahead and sit down." About ten minutes later, Abby came back with the maître d' in tow. I couldn't believe my eyes. The maître d' spoke briefly with some people at a ringside table. They gradually rose and walked away. He then came and got us and escorted us to the vacated table. I later saw the people who had been at ringside seated at our old table. It embarrassed the life out of all of us. Abby, however, looked pleased as punch. Years later, I asked Abby how he managed to pull that off. He said, "It was easy, Don. I gave the maître d' a hundred-dollar bill." But I wasn't sure I believed him. I just couldn't see ol' penurious Abby laying out a hundred dollars cash for anything.

As I recall, I stayed with Abby for about six years before I moved on to another agent, but I missed him. Abby was colorful and interesting, and in spite of all his shenanigans, he was a damn good agent. I am presently represented by a very good agent, Barry Freed.

Barney Fife and Other

A publicity still from _Wake Me When It's Over_

Our Final Season

New technologies were suddenly taking place in television. Beginning with our very first show from downtown Burbank, we went on tape and the laugh track was added to our audience reaction. I was delighted with the sense of security the new technologies gave us. At the same time, I began to worry that they were diminishing the quality of our work. For example, when I questioned whether or not a certain joke would work, the answer was often, "Don't worry about it. The laugh track will love it." I also felt that being on tape took away some of the excitement that was generated in the old live shows in New York. But there was no question about it, we were working in a more relaxed atmosphere, and I was certainly grateful for that. In any case, it turned out to be our last season.

During this final season, Mervyn LeRoy called and asked me to do him a favor. He wanted to test Dick Shawn for one of the leads in a picture he was about to do called *Wake Me When It's Over,* and he asked me if I would do one of the parts in Dick's screen test. It turned out to be a good test for Dick, and he got the role. It turned out to be a good test for me also, because a short time later, Mervyn LeRoy called and asked me to do the part I did for the test in the movie. It was just a small supporting role, but I was always happy to be working in a feature. LeRoy agreed to work around my *Steve Allen* schedule. We shot the picture at Twentieth Century Fox, and our major star was Ernie Kovacs. I enjoyed meeting Ernie. He was a very interesting man. Unfortunately, the picture wasn't a hit, but so goes the movie business.

A Wondrous Turn of Events

As we neared the end of our *Steve Allen* run, I began casting about for future employment. One night, Kay and I were playing bridge with Pat Harrington and his wife at their home when Pat, who was up for a part on the *Danny Thomas* TV series, asked if we could stop playing to watch Danny's show. He turned it on and much to my surprise, Andy Griffith was the guest star that night. Pat told me the show they were doing was actually the pilot for a new series which would star Andy Griffith as a small-town sheriff. In the show, Danny drove through a small town and Sheriff Andy Taylor gave him a ticket. It was a wonderful episode and Andy was absolutely delightful.

The wheels in my brain began to whirl. I had been out of touch with Andy for some time, but I knew he was in New York doing a Broadway musical called *Destry Rides Again*. I called Andy the next day. I told him how much I enjoyed the show. Then I said, "Listen, don't you think Sheriff Andy Taylor ought to have a deputy?" There was a long pause. Then Andy said, "That's a hell of an idea. Tell you what, I'll mention it to our executive producer. His name is Sheldon Leonard. Wait a couple of days and give him a call."

A week later I was in Sheldon Leonard's office. Sheldon was a pleasant man who spoke with measured deliberateness. He was famous for his verbosity. He was presently the executive producer of *The Danny Thomas Show* and was on his way to becoming one of the most powerful producers in television. He prodded me with questions about what I thought this deputy character should be like. I had no preconceived ideas, but we kicked it around for the better part of an hour, and when he dismissed me, he told me that the possibility of adding a deputy to the cast would be taken under advisement.

We did the final *Steve Allen Show,* and I waited anxiously to hear from the Andy Griffith people. Finally, after three weeks of waiting by that phone again, Sherwin called and said they had made an offer. I almost fainted with delight. I had a good feeling about this. A real good feeling, even before it started.

aracters I Have Known

A Fantastic Beginning

The day I sat down with the cast to read aloud the script of the first *Andy Griffith Show* was one of the most delightful days of my life. I was, of course, already at ease with Andy, and I loved the rest of the cast. The first show was centered around Andy, Aunt Bee, and Opie. It was a warm, wonderful script. I was very impressed with Frances Bavier and little Ronny Howard, who, at the age of five, was already such a good actor it was hard to believe. Our producer and head writer, Aaron Ruben, looked like he was going to be a lot of fun. On top of all these good things, I was happy to be leaving the variety-show format behind and heading into film. *The Andy Griffith Show* would be filmed with one camera just like a movie.

Our schedule was laid out like this: at nine on Thursday morning, the cast would read down the script for the following week. We would then read aloud the script for the week after that. This would be followed by a discussion with Sheldon Leonard, Aaron Ruben, and the director regarding possible changes in the script. The cast would then be dismissed. Aaron Ruben, the director, and Andy would spend the rest of the afternoon on rewrites. We would spend the entire day on Friday rehearsing on the set. We learned our lines on the weekend, and began shooting at eight o'clock on Monday morning. We filmed for three full days—Monday, Tuesday, and Wednesday.

In that first show, my character, Barney Fife, was referred to as Andy's cousin. This idea was dropped after the first few episodes and it was never alluded to again. The second show, called "Manhunt," gave Barney full rein. It was filled with wonderful comedy and I took to it like a duck takes to water. This

An early publicity shot of Andy and me

episode was written by Chuck Stewart and Jack Elinson. A great deal of Barney Fife's character was set in that show. It was in this show that Chuck and Jack established the wonderful running gag whereby Andy allows Barney to carry only one bullet.

We filmed eight or ten shows before we went on the air, but I don't think there was ever a doubt in Andy's mind or in mine during those first weeks shooting that we would be a hit. It just felt right, it just felt good. When we hit the air, it wasn't long before we hit the top ten and we never fell out of it.

Andy Griffith

Once again, Andy Griffith was having the time of his life. His enthusiasm and sense of fun was catching, and the set crackled with it all day long. You never saw a happier cast in your life. We were having fun. I couldn't wait to go to work in the morning. The star of the show always sets the tone, and Andy certainly set a wonderful tone in this one.

Besides being the star, Andy owned the major share of the show, and that made him the boss. And he was a good boss. It was clear right from the beginning that he was a conscientious, tireless worker who kept his eye on the script and the cast and the crew. Very little escaped Andy's notice.

Andy Griffith is a consummate actor. His work as Lonesome Rhodes in the motion picture *A Face in the Crowd* is proof of that. Andy's portrayal of Andy Taylor seemed so natural, you forgot he was acting. In order to believe Mayberry and some of its strangely funny citizens, the viewer first had to believe that this

Barney Fife on his motorcycle

dependable sheriff was holding everything together. In the first few episodes, Andy played Andy Taylor in a broader, more comedic way, but Andy said he soon realized that the sheriff had to be a solid citizen, and let Barney Fife and others do most of the comedy.

Chemistry between Andy and me on camera clicked in almost immediately, and we began working together like hand and glove. When Andy assumed the role of straight man in scenes between the two of us, there was none better in the business. His timing was immaculate.

Another thing about Andy that spurred *me* on was the fact

Behind the scenes in Mayberry

that he was such a good audience for Barney. When I did Barney
Fife, I truly broke Andy up. Quite often, when I was doing something funny, I could see in Andy's eyes that he was fighting to
keep from laughing, and that made me all the funnier.

An important thing for Andy and me and the show began to
happen early on. We both loved the idea of shooting a scene every
now and then in which Andy and Barney would just sit and shoot
the breeze about something that had nothing whatsoever to do

114

Joanna Moore played
Andy's girlfriend

with the story we were doing. This was met with some resistance at first, but it soon became clear that our audience loved it.

A few weeks into the first season, Andy invited me to sit in on the rewrite sessions. I thoroughly enjoyed participating in these. There was no one better on script that Aaron Ruben, but Andy was developing a pretty keen eye for editing himself. He insisted on keeping the dialogue as true to life as possible. He used to say, "If it sounds like a joke, throw it out." One time, when he was criticizing a line in the script, he said, "I knew a fellow back home who was like this fellow here, and he wouldn't say it like that." He also had a good eye for stories, and he sat in

aracters I Have Known

with Aaron and the writers before each season, when they kicked around story ideas.

Quite often, when a page or two had been cut out of the script for one reason or another, Andy would turn to me and say, "Why don't you go over there in the corner and write us a comedy bit." Every once in a while I'd come up with a good one and Andy would laugh and clap his hands. There was one thing for sure about Andy, you never had to guess whether or not he was tickled. When something broke him up, he would roar with laughter, clap his hands, and hit the wall or the desk or whatever was in front of him. If he was *really* tickled, he would whoop and holler and take off running. His wife once told me, "Don't ever sit in front of Andy in a movie theater. If he gets tickled with something, he's liable to hit you right on the head."

I'll never forget one occasion when I broke Andy up. Andy had once told me an amusing thing his father used to do when he would buy Andy a suit back in North Carolina. While the clerk was wrapping his suit, his dad would sidle up to the clerk and say, in a conspiratorial tone, "You don't suppose you could throw in a pair of black socks with that, do you?" Well, one day Andy asked me to go shopping for clothes with him in Beverly Hills, and we went to one of those ritzy clothing stores on Rodeo Drive. Andy bought a whole wardrobe: suits, jackets, and slacks. While the sophisticated clerk was tallying up the bill, I leaned over confidentially, and said, "You don't suppose you could throw in a pair of black silk socks with that, do you?" Well, Andy let out a whoop and took off running through the store, knocking down racks and displays, and everything in his path. I thought the poor clerk was going to have a heart attack.

Andy and I continued to get along great, although we didn't socialize a great deal, probably because we spent so much time together at the studio.

Andy has a playful side and he loves to tease. My full name is Jesse Donald Knotts, and when Andy found out I didn't care much for my first name, he started calling me Jess, and he calls me that to this day. I started calling him Ange both on and off camera. I don't know where that came from.

We worked together so well, I once asked Andy if he'd like to team up for good. He politely and understandably declined. An actor with Andy's range could never consider tying himself to a comedy team.

Our Director, Bob Sweeney

I've often wondered how Sheldon Leonard managed to put so many talented people together for one show. We were blessed with the best in every department—writing, directing, and acting. Our producer and head writer, Aaron Ruben, worked beautifully with the writers and ran the show with humor and skill. Once in a while, Aaron would write a script for the show. Aaron's scripts would always be among the best of the season. Most of our scripts were written by the teams of Chuck Stewart and Jack Elinson, Jim Fritzell and Everett Greenbaum, Harvey Bullock and Ray Allen, and Sam Bobrick and Bill Idelson. Needless to say, they were all excellent writers.

The first ten shows were directed by Don Weiss. Then Bob Sweeney came on board to direct for the next three years. Bruce Bilson was our first assistant director. How fortunate we were to get Bob Sweeney. Bob came to the show with experience in almost every field of comedy. He had been an actor, a director,

Andy and me fooling around

and a comic. As a director, Bob had the ability to reach down and get the very best you had, and he wouldn't settle until you had given him your very best. Bob had a wonderful sense of humor and he had a good feel for when Andy and I were right on in a scene. When Bob would yell, "Cut and print!" after a take, we knew we had done it right. Bob also had a feel for the warm scenes. He worked beautifully with little Ronny and Frances Bavier, and he knew how to tug at the audience's heartstrings.

Sometimes Bob's humor had a mischievous streak in it, and he loved to get my goat. We once had a scene in which a bunch of chickens were supposed to fly right into Barney and get him all upset. Bob had a fellow just off-camera to throw the chickens

at me. Bob heard me tell the fellow to throw the chickens at me chest high. I didn't care to get hit in the face. Bob whispered to the fellow, "No, I want you to hit him right in the face with every chicken," and that's what the fellow did. I was furious. Bob Sweeney was hysterical, and he also got exactly what he wanted on film.

Another time, I was supposed to step out in the street in front of a car, almost getting hit, and Bob kept shooting it over, insisting that I never let the car get close enough to me. I said, "You don't care whose life you risk, do you?" He said, "Don, there's a stunt driver in that car. He's not going to hit you." I could see that he was bubbling with laughter somewhere inside of him. He had the devil in his eyes. Finally, he took the driver aside and told him to speed up at the last minute on the next take. That time the car came so close to me I almost fainted. I was furious, and I started screaming at Sweeney. I looked over and he was lying on the ground behind the camera laughing his head off.

Bob Sweeney left the show at the end of the third season. We missed Sween, but some very fine directors stepped in. Most of the shows during the next two seasons were directed by Alan Rafkin, Coby Ruskin, and Jeffrey Hayden.

My friend Andy Griffith and me

Stunt Man, Please

I was never very brave when it came to taking chances on film. I've heard all these stories about guys doing their own stunts and so on. Not me! One time, in a sketch on *The Steve Allen Show,* I was supposed to walk into a big lion's cage with a real lion in there. "You don't have to worry about that lion," the trainer had told me. "He's old and tired, and doesn't even have all his teeth." Well, in our first camera rehearsal, I started to open the door to go into the cage, when I looked over and saw

Andy and I are joined by Jerry Van Dyke

that the trainer had a gun aimed at the lion. "Hold it!" I cried, "If you're not worried about the lion, why do you have a gun aimed at him?" "Oh," he said, "well, of course, you never know." "That's it!" I yelled, "I'm not going in there." And I didn't. Gabe Dell replaced me in the sketch. Gene Autry was a guest on the show that week, and he told me he didn't blame me. He said he once did a movie in which an actor was supposed to wrestle with a bear. The trainer told the actor, "You don't have to worry, this bear won't hurt you. Look." With that, he slapped the bear's face playfully, and the bear proceeded to bite the trainer's nose off!

There's actually a lot of real danger working in front of a movie camera, and you do have to look out for yourself. One experience early on in Hollywood taught me that lesson loud and clear. I was asked to do a part in a short film for charity, a cowboy movie starring Randolph Scott. There was a scene in which I was to stand in front of a wooden fence, while Scott was shooting at me. They screwed these tiny explosives called squibs into the fence. They detonate the squibs electronically, blowing out tiny holes. It looks like the shots are going into the wood. I was quite near the squibs, so I asked, "Is this safe?" The special-effects man said, "Oh, sure! We've scored the wood. It'll blow out as dust." Well, Scott started shooting, the squibs exploded and one blew a two-inch long splinter right into my ear. I had to go to the infirmary to have it removed. The doctor said, "If it weren't for the curve of the ear canal, you'd have lost your hearing in that ear."

Years later, in another western, *The Apple Dumpling Gang,* Tim Conway was inadvertently supposed to set my handkerchief on fire. I had it in my back pocket. The special-effects man wanted to be sure it would burn, so he soaked it in kerosene. Tim lit the hankie and I went up in flames. The director rushed in and threw me on the ground to beat out the fire before I roasted.

Later, Tim and I were shooting *The Apple Dumping Gang* sequel in the desert near Canaab, Utah. I had a scene in which we were court-marshaled by the army and put in an old-time, horse-drawn patrol wagon. They wanted to lock us in, but Tim said, with my full approval, "Don't *really* lock us in, because the horses might take off for that big cliff over there." They said okay and gave the horses a slap. Sure enough, the horses took off, full speed, straight for the cliff. We were about to jump out when a wrangler rode up and stopped the horses just short of the abyss.

Barney Fife and Other

A Superb Cast

I can't say enough about the cast on *The Andy Griffith Show*. There wasn't a weak actor in the lot, and they brought a great deal of experience to the show. Betty Lynn (Thelma Lou) had been featured in dozens of motion pictures for all the major studios. Hal Smith had been in great demand in radio and television for years. Frances Bavier was known to theater audiences in New York and had compiled a list of credits in television. Elinor Donahue, Andy Taylor's first girlfriend, had been a star on *Father Knows Best*. Aneta Corsaut and Joanna Moore, who subsequently played Andy's girlfriends, also arrived with extensive backgrounds in television. Howard McNear had logged years and years in radio, television, and the theater. Even Ronny Howard had compiled a list of credits at the grand old age of five. George Lindsey, who came on later to play Goober, also had a thriving television background. The only one who may have lacked experience was Jim Nabors, who joined us in our third season to play Gomer. Jim was so packed with natural talent, he didn't need a lot of experience.

Jim Nabors was discovered in a little nightclub in Santa Monica called The Horn, where he was performing nightly. We all knew the owner there, Rick Ricardi. Rick got hold of Andy's manager, Dick Linke, and told him he'd better come over and have a look at this guy. Dick was impressed and he took Andy to see him. When Andy told me about Jim, he was really excited. He kept saying, "You can't believe this guy." Soon afterward, Jim joined the cast of *The Andy Griffith Show*. Jim's character, Gomer Pyle, added so much to the show, and I enjoyed doing comedy scenes with him. I don't know who thought up Gomer

Jim Nabors and me

and Goober, but they were a couple of funny pistols. Jim left our show at the end of the fourth season to do *Gomer Pyle, U.S.M.C.*, and Aaron Ruben went with him to produce the new series. Bob Ross came in to take Aaron's place. During the hiatus period, before Jim started work on his new series, Andy and Jim and I got up an act and played Harrah's in Lake Tahoe. We had a blast. Jim and Andy each did solo singing spots, we all did a little comedy and then closed with the three of us harmonizing some spirituals. I'm afraid I was a little out of my league with those two voices, but I managed to blend in a little tenor with Jim singing high tenor over me. I'm not one to brag, but I have to say we tore it up. William Morris was so impressed, they sold the show to

George Lindsey, Andy, Jack Dodson, and I try out some crazy costumes

CBS for a television special. Andy and I often commiserated about our early days as live entertainers. Neither of us enjoyed it that much, but we did enjoy that shot at Harrah's. Several years later, we decided to do it again. This time, we took Jerry Van Dyke with us. Jerry does one of the funniest nightclub routines you'll ever see. We did two weeks at Caesar's Palace in Las Vegas, and then three weeks at Harrah's. It was a lot of fun, but we haven't played a nightclub since.

I have to say a word about Howard McNear. Howard was one of the funniest comic actors I ever worked with. I put him right up there with Tim Conway. I cannot tell you how many takes I ruined, breaking up at Howard. You never knew which look or gesture or reading you were going to get from Howard, and he usually caught you completely off guard. I love to listen to old radio shows, and Howard's voice shows up on so many of them. What a treat he was!

The first year Ron Howard did Opie, he was a preschooler and couldn't even read. Ron's father, Rance, also an actor, helped Ron memorize his lines. Ron's folks were wonderful parents. They, of course, brought Ron to the set and their handling of Ron could not have been better. Rance and Ron obviously had a wonderful father-son relationship, and Ron was the best-behaved child actor I ever worked with. Most kid actors, quite frankly, are a pain in the neck. Not Ron. I can't remember ever seeing him get out of line. When he was working, he was right there, diligent and concentrated. When he wasn't on-camera, you didn't even know he was around. I think Ron's becoming a director took most of us by surprise. It certainly did me, anyway. Ron was such a natural actor, I guess I assumed he would continue acting when he grew up. During a personal appearance, George Lindsey was asked what he thought of Ron's success as a director. George said, "We call him Mr. Howard now." Andy and I recently met in New York to do *Good Morning America*. While we were there, we went to visit Ron at the studio where he was shooting the movie *Ransom*. It was a kick watching him direct. It was certainly no surprise to see that he was right at home. He is, incidentally, every bit as nice a man as he was a little boy. And that's no surprise either.

Howard Morris did a phenomenal portrayal of the character Ernest T. Bass. He actually appears in only five episodes, but anybody who has ever followed the *Andy Griffith* series can tell you all about Ernest T. Bass, the wild man from up in the mountains. The episode in which Howard appeared was built around a mountain family called the Darlings. Also featured in that episode were Denver Pyle, Maggie Peterson, and a bluegrass musical group, The Dillards. Howard is very popular on Mayberry

Barney Fife and Other

personal appearances, and I am asked about Ernest T. wherever I go. Howie eventually became a director and wound up directing several episodes of *The Andy Griffith Show*. He had made his mark early on as an outstanding supporting comic on the old Sid Caesar and Imogene Coca variety series, *Your Show of Shows*.

An Unusual Makeup Man

One gentleman who added a lot of fun to our off-camera time on *The Andy Griffith Show* was our makeup man, Lee Greenway. Lee, a soft-spoken southerner in his forties, was a man of many talents. In addition to his artistry in makeup, Lee was a world champion skeet shooter, a shrewd horse trader, and a fine musician. He played the five-string banjo. He kept his banjo on the set, and Andy and I had a lot of fun harmonizing to Lee's accompaniment.

One day, I got a firsthand view of Lee's acumen as a horse trader. I mentioned casually that I had just bought a new golf bag. Like a shot, Lee asked, "What did you do with your old bag?" "Well, it's in the trunk of my car," I said. Lee said, "I'll give you twenty-five dollars cash for it right now, sight unseen." I stammered, "Well, I uh . . ." Lee took the money out of his pocket. "Cash right now." The next thing I knew, the two of us were opening the trunk of my car and I was handing Lee my old golf bag. My guess is he already had a buyer in mind.

I think one of the things that endeared Lee to all of us was his sense of humor. And there was no end to Lee Greenway stories in the company. One day, Lee was working on the lawn in front of his house when a woman passing by stopped to admire his work. "My goodness," she said, "that lawn looks absolutely beautiful. I don't know what a person would have to do to get someone to do such wonderful work on your yard." Lee pointed to his house and said, "That woman in there sleeps with me."

Lee and Andy became close friends and Lee taught Andy the fine points of skeet shooting.

Our prop man, Reggie Smith, was an interesting man. Reggie was a wonderful cook, and every one in a while he'd cook a delicious lunch for three or four of us in the prop room. Reggie belonged to a nudist colony and we kidded him quite a bit about that. I got a good laugh one Friday afternoon when I hollered, "Everyone's going away for the weekend, and Reggie's the only one who doesn't have to pack."

Gaining Perspective

A short time after we finished filming the first season's shows, I got the surprise of my life. I was in my backyard painting our fence when I was called to the telephone. I was greeted on the phone with congratulations. I had been nominated for an Emmy for best supporting actor. I was stunned. This was something that had never crossed my mind. I was even more stunned when I won. I got an unexpected laugh during my acceptance speech, when I said I had nothing to say because I had always been a prepared loser. But it was a good feeling and I must confess that for the first time in my career, I felt like strutting a little bit.

Dick Powell presents me with my Emmy

The next day, I decided to play golf and I strutted my way over to the golf club. Why not? My picture was in the paper and everything. I was told there was a guy on the first tee looking for a game. I walked out to the tee and approached the stranger with my hand out. "Hi, there," I said magnanimously, "I'm Don Knotts." "Glad to know you," said the man, "Bill Smith. I'm in hardware, what's your line?" I made a note never to strut.

I never got to know Peter Falk very well, but I did get a glimpse of his sense of humor, a trait for which he is widely know in Hollywood. When I won my second Emmy, Falk was my presenter. He was the one who opened the envelope and read my name. Two or three weeks after the Emmys, I was sitting in a supper club in New York City when I spotted Peter Falk at a nearby table. He was trying to get my attention. When he saw that I was looking at him, he mouthed the words, "You didn't win."

A Successful Lot

The sound stage where we shot all the interiors for *The Andy Griffith Show* was on a Desilu lot located in Hollywood. Desilu was a company owned by Desi Arnaz and Lucille Ball. It was a small lot with just a few sound stages, but it was a busy and exciting lot. In addition to our show, the lot housed *The Danny Thomas Show* and *The Dick Van Dyke Show*, and later on, *I Spy*, starring Bill Cosby and Robert Culp, and *The Joey Bishop Show*. The man at the helm of all these shows was Sheldon Leonard.

The Dick Van Dyke Show did not do too well in the ratings

Me in Miami

in its first season, and General Foods wanted to cancel it. Sheldon Leonard was convinced the show would climb into the top
ten in the second season, and he flew back East to convince General Foods. They okayed a second season, and as we all know,

The Dick Van Dyke Show became one of the top programs on television.

One day, I went over to watch them rehearse. Unlike *The Andy Griffith Show, The Dick Van Dyke Show* was shot with multicameras in front of an audience. I sat down next to Carl Reiner in the audience seats. Carl was the producer and head writer of the show. I turned to Carl, and asked, "What's Dick like? I don't know him." Carl said, "You want to know how nice Dick Van Dyke is? I'll tell you. You're a nice guy, Don. He's nicer."

Mary Tyler Moore came by our sound stage once in a while to watch us work. I really admired her comedic talent.

A Special Special

Shortly before we hit the air in the third year, General Foods decided to do a special with all the stars who would be working for them in the coming season. Can you imagine a lineup like this today? The show starred Jack Benny, Danny Thomas, Dick Van Dyke, Andy Griffith, Lucille Ball, and Phil Silvers. I couldn't believe my own good fortune. A clever running gag had been written into the show using my nervous character. I felt like I was in the Land of Oz with these heavyweights. I mean, they were the greatest comedians on earth! And boy, did I learn a lot! The learning began right at the reading table. Jack Benny and Lucille Ball were the heaviest in the show. After the reading, they started the process of editing. They weeded their way through the script with such meticulous care you wouldn't believe. Every line, every word was evaluated, and very subtle changes were made. It was fascinating. Jack Benny was famous in the business for his editing ability, and watching him work was a real learning experience. He was so precise. Nothing was left to chance. Lucille Ball was no slouch at it herself. I had to leave after a few hours, and they were still at it when I walked out the door.

The rehearsals for that show were a riot. Jack Benny was full of fun, and he kept everybody laughing. He was clearly enjoying himself, but by the time we were within a day or so of taping the show, he became noticeably tense. He started worrying about his material, and he asked everybody if they thought his stuff was funny. I had always heard that he was a worrier, but that didn't surprise me. I had observed that most good comedians worry a great deal about their material. The night before the taping, Benny said, "You know, I'm not feeling well, I may be coming down with the flu." The show played like a house afire and, of course, Jack Benny's stuff got screams from the audience just as we all knew it would. After the show, I asked, "How are you feeling, Mr. Benny?" He looked at me quizzically and said, "What? Oh . . . fine, great. Never felt better in my life."

The Great Red Skelton

TV half-hour comedies today do twenty-two to twenty-four episodes a season. In the days of *The Andy Griffith Show,* we did thirty-two. That still gave us plenty of time off, and I picked up a good bit of work during those hiatus periods. I appeared on several specials and variety shows. One in particular gave me a special thrill. It was *The Red Skelton Show*. Red Skelton was one of our all-time great comics. Like Jimmy Durante, he had a warmth that came through to the audience. His television show on CBS remained in the top ten for several years. He was still in the top ten, in fact, when, in a surprising sudden move, CBS pulled Red's show off the air, along with several other longtime favorites, including *Mayberry RFD*. Red was devastated.

I appeared as a guest on *The Red Skelton Show* twice, and I was delighted with the opportunity to get to know the great comedian. I remember the first time I sat at the table to read down the script with Red and the company. Red remarked, "Oh, boy, another night with no sleep." Later, during rehearsal, I said, "Gee, Red, I'm sorry you have so much trouble sleeping." "Oh, no," he said laughing, "I sleep like a baby, but I don't want them to know it. I don't want them to think, 'He makes all that money, and he sleeps too!' " And then he roared with laughter. I didn't know if he was putting them on or me, but I didn't really care. The whole notion was just so damn funny.

Red was a lot of fun and he had a mischievous streak. His dress rehearsals became legendary because he would substitute innuendo and outright dirty jokes for the real dialogue. People from all over CBS would come to sit in the audience for those dress rehearsals.

Red was famous for his personal library of jokes. Apparently, he had quite a collection. One day, I told him a joke I had remembered from an old movie: a fellow walks up to a guy in a small town, and says, "I'm a stranger in town. Can you tell me a good place to eat?" The guy says, "Sure, the Palmer House in Chicago." Red laughed, and said, "That's funny, I'll use that sometime." Without telling me, he worked it into the show that very night with one of the other actors. It got a good laugh and Red looked at me with a big, wide grin.

Barney Fife and Other

Having come up the hard way through burlesque and vaudeville, Red had a great appreciation for making money. One day, he said, "Don, do you ever work state fairs?" I told him I did not. He pulled a check out of his pocket and showed it to me. It was made out to Red Skelton for $25,000. "I made that just last night in Ohio," he said. "Get your agent on that."

Red Skelton was one of a kind. On a nightclub stage he could make you laugh and he could make you cry. There's no way you could watch Red Skelton without being moved. He was just great! There's no other word.

A Rap with Hedda Hopper

One day, after I'd done the *Griffith* show for three or four years, I got on an airplane in New York bound for L.A., and was surprised to find myself seated next to the renowned columnist Hedda Hopper. We had a nice chat over lunch. She told me that when my run with the *Griffith* show was over, I should take some time off and go to Europe. "Don't worry," she said, "they won't forget you." But she spent most of the time asking me questions. She was interviewing me, though I didn't know it until her column came out the next day. After a while, she excused herself and went to sleep.

A fellow then tapped me on the shoulder and identified himself as a motion picture PR man. "Do you suppose you could introduce me to Miss Hopper?" he asked. "I want to invite her to a studio screening of *Lolita*." I said, "Sure." I wondered how Miss Hopper would react to the invitation. She had always taken a

135

strong stance against anything even bordering on immorality in movies. As we were landing, I introduced him. We pulled to the gate and he started helping her with her bags. He said, "By the way, Miss Hopper, we are screening *Lolita,* and we'd like you to be our guest." She threw him a disdainful look, turned, and started down the aisle toward the exit. Over her shoulder she said, "I read *Lolita* while I was in Egypt and I threw it in the Nile."

Mr. Limpet

I was beginning to compile a pretty good list of motion picture credits. I landed a part in a Doris Day picture, *Move Over Darling,* and a cameo in *Mad, Mad, Mad, Mad World,* which used every comedian in Hollywood. Finally a break came my way that eventually led to a five-year motion picture contract. I was offered the starring role of Henry Limpet in a motion picture called *Mr. Limpet,* which was finally titled *The Incredible Mr. Limpet.* I think it was the first feature motion picture ever to combine live action with extensive animation. The story was a fantasy about a man who loved fish so much that he jumped or fell (we're not quite sure which) into the ocean and became one and, as a fish, led an attack against the German navy in World War II. I was only on-screen as myself for about twenty minutes. The rest of my work was doing the voice of the animated fish. The picture was produced for Warner Brothers by a man named John C. Rose. Rose was a thorough and tireless worker. A perfectionist, he hired and fired several animation artists before he found one

Carole Cook and me in *The Incredible Mr. Limpet*

who came up with a drawing of the fish, Henry Limpet, that satisfied him.

The movie was adapted from a book called *Mr. Limpet*. John Rose didn't like the title. He said there were too many shows around called *Mr. This* or *Mr. That*. He searched for a new title for almost a year before he got the idea to put the word *Incredible* before *Mr. Limpet*.

I don't think the powers that be at the studio quite understood the picture. According to the director, Arthur Luben, Jack Warner, who'd been watching the dailies, sent him a memo one day that read: "You've got a funny actor down there. Why don't you give him something funny to do?" Mr. Limpet was not supposed to be funny. Quaint and amusing, yes, but not funny. All of John Rose's dogged determination paid off. I thought it turned out to be a splendid motion picture. I can't say the New York critics agreed with that assessment, however. They panned it. While I was in New York doing PR for the picture, I approached the front door of a restaurant, and the doorman said, "Welcome back to New York, Mr. Knotts. Gee, I understand you've got a lousy movie in town."

A number of things went wrong with the picture's distribution. John Rose had been working hard to get the picture into the Radio City Music Hall in New York. Apparently, the Music Hall people were considering it for an Easter release. The story I heard was that they decided against it because the name Don Knotts did not have a motion picture track record. Apparently lacking faith in the movie, Warner Brothers released it without much fanfare and at first it didn't do well at all. But it gradually picked up steam and became so popular over the years and such a perennial favorite on television that Warner Brothers recently announced their intention to do a remake of it, starring Jim Carrey.

A Tough Decision

It was *The Incredible Mr. Limpet* that caught the attention of Lou Wasserman, then president of Universal, and led to a motion picture contract for me, which brings me to the reason I left *The Andy Griffith Show* when I did. I left the show after five seasons, and Andy continued on for three more, completing an eight-year run. I do personal appearances from time to time, and at the end of my show I take questions from the audience. With-

The Incredible Mr. Limpet

out fail, I am asked why I left *The Andy Griffith Show* at the end of five seasons. The answer is simply this: Andy had always insisted that he would never go beyond five years, so during our fifth year, I naturally thought it might be a good idea to start looking around for another job. I began meeting people at the studios and networks, and since I was pretty hot at the time, I started getting some pretty attractive television offers. Suddenly I landed an interview that really made me sit up and take notice. It was with Lou Wasserman at Universal, and he wanted to talk to me about a picture contract. When I sat down with him, he told me that he had run *The Incredible Mr. Limpet* and that was the

Jack Weston and me in a scene from *Mr. Limpet*

reason he wanted to talk to me. He was very impressed with the picture. He told me that if Disney had made it and promoted it the way they do, it would have been a blockbuster. He offered me a five-year contract. He said he wanted to build my name in family motion picture comedies. He offered me free rein. He said I could pick my own screenwriters and decide on my own pictures. This was an offer I could hardly refuse. Remember, there was no such thing as television when I was growing up. Motion pictures were my dream.

It was along about this time that Andy told me he had changed his mind and he had decided to stay on another three years. It's true that I had not yet signed a contract with Universal, but I had made a verbal commitment and my mind was pretty set on trying to start a picture career. This was an opportunity that might never present itself again. It was tough to leave the show, of course. It had been the richest and most rewarding experience of my entire life. A defining event. I wondered if I would ever have that much fun again.

The First Screenplay

I had no idea what my first picture at Universal should be about. I began running possibilities through my mind and one day, for some reason, a particular episode of *The Andy Griffith Show* jumped out at me. It was the one where Andy and Gomer and Barney went into a haunted house. I thought to myself, people seem to enjoy the idea of seeing me get scared. So a picture built around a haunted house ought to be right down my alley. I pieced together the rough thread of a story, and I thought it might be getting close to time to start talking to some writers. We were nearing the end of the *Griffith* season, and I asked Jim Fritzell and Everett Greenbaum if they would be interested in working with me on a screenplay during the show's hiatus. They said they would, and Universal put them under contract.

I got a wonderful break. Lou Wasserman assigned Ed Montagne to produce the picture. Ed was producing a hit television series for Universal called *McHale's Navy,* which starred Ernest Borgnine, Tim Conway, and Joe Flynn. Ed was a knowledgeable film producer and one of the nicest men you'll ever meet. He asked Jim and Everett and me to meet with him in his office.

Ed's office was on the ninth floor of the executive tower. This caused an unusual and amusing wrinkle right off the bat. Jim

The Incredible Mr. Limpet

Fritzell was acrophobic, and he would die before he would go up to the ninth floor. Everett and I went up without him. We sat down in Ed's office, and Ed said, "Where's Jim?" "Well, sir," I said, "there seems to be a slight problem. You see, Jim can't come up to the ninth floor." Ed was understandably puzzled. "You see," I went on, "Jim is acrophobic." Ed looked at me for a long time, and then he stared into space, and finally he turned and looked out the window for a while. It really was kind of funny. Finally, he turned back to us, and said, "Where do you suggest we meet?" "Well," I said, "we thought maybe there was an empty office downstairs someplace." Ed went out and talked to his secretary, and they made a few calls, and finally he came back and said that he had indeed located an empty office in the basement. We took the elevator down to the basement and Everett went out, got Jim, and brought him in.

Ed had already studied our story idea. "Boys," he said, "we've got a tough job ahead of us. We're combining a comedy and a mystery here, and we've got to carefully construct this story." After the meeting, I got a bright idea. Remembering what a good story constructionist Andy Griffith is, I called Andy and asked if he would consider helping us put this story together. He said he'd be happy to. I called Ed Montagne and he arranged for Universal to pay Andy a token compensation for helping us.

The five of us sat down in that little basement office every day for the next two weeks and hammered out the story outline for a motion picture that would eventually be called *The Ghost and Mr. Chicken*. I was so proud of us. It was a damn good story. Universal then provided me with an office, and Jim and Everett and I sat down to write the screenplay. Jim and Everett wrote most of it, of course, but I put my two cents in. I had a ball working with these two guys. They were full of fun. Jim was more the constructionist, getting you from point A to point B, but Ev-

Jack Weston

erett was one of the wittiest men I had ever known. I had met Jim and Everett years before, back in New York when they were writing the *Mr. Peepers* TV series, which starred Wally Cox. I did a bit part on *Mr. Peepers*.

I don't remember exactly how long it took us to write the movie script, but I would guess it was in the neighborhood of three months. In any case, I never laughed so much in my life. Everett would come up with lines right out of the blue that would knock you off your seat. He also had an infectious cackle that was familiar to all his friends, and he had a multitude of friends. Everett became a much-loved character in the business. He switched careers in his later years, incidentally, and turned to acting. He became quite successful at it.

Besides having laughed my head off every day, I was thrilled with the result of our work. We had followed the outline faithfully, and packed it full of funny lines and situations. One of Andy Griffith's suggestions, incidentally, turned out to be a gem. If you have seen the movie, you'll remember that Everett keeps shouting from off-camera, "Atta boy, Luther!" (which is my name in the picture). In the original outline, Jim and Everett had written in "Atta boy, Luther" only once. That was in the scene in the park where Luther is trying to deliver a speech. Remembering what fun the audience had with the running gag using Juanita, Barney Fife's telephone girlfriend, whom the audience never sees, Andy suggested we continue the "Atta boy, Luther" throughout the picture as a running gag. It really paid off. For years after the picture was released, people yelled "Atta boy, Luther" when they saw me on the street.

Preproduction

Ed Montagne was very pleased with the script and he sent it upstairs to Lou Wasserman. A few days later, we got the nod, and Ed set the wheels in motion for preproduction. The working title Jim and Everett had used for the movie was *Running Scared,* but this title was not available. It was Everett who finally came up with *The Ghost and Mr. Chicken,* which I thought was an ingenious title.

Ed Montagne let me sit in with him on some of the preproduction. It was fascinating. I went with him around the lot, picking out locations for the outdoor scenes, and talking with the set designer for the interiors. I got my two cents in on the kind of courtroom I wanted. I was after a real small-town courtroom with ceiling fans. The set designer said he could handle that.

My leading lady in *The Ghost and Mr. Chicken* was the lovely Joan Staley

Ed was really good at casting. He had been around the film business all his life, and he knew all the actors in Hollywood. He wanted my input, so I sat with him on some of the actors' interviews. This was certainly an eye-opener for me. I had never sat on this side of the casting couch. It was very interesting. Some of the actors were very nervous, but Ed always managed to put them at ease. Ed had a genuine affection for actors. I saw that casting was a long, tiresome, and sometimes frustrating process, but Ed was skilled at it and, in the end, he came up with what I thought was a very fine cast.

I got a shock when Ed handed me our shooting schedule. It gave us exactly seventeen shooting days. I couldn't believe it! Less than three and a half weeks to shoot a feature motion picture! Unbelievable! Well, this called for some fast work, and some long hours. I asked Ed if we could get Alan Rafkin to direct the picture. I always got along well with Alan on the *Griffith* show, and I thought he was a good director. He was fast, efficient, and he was a lot of fun. Alan has a great sense of humor, and I thought if *anyone* could shoot a picture in seventeen days, Alan Rafkin could. Universal made a deal with Alan, and I was much relieved.

A fine actress named Joan Staley was set to play my leading lady. Joan was under contract to Universal, so as soon as some of the sets were built, I rehearsed what scenes I could with her. They seemed to go well and I was very pleased with Joan. I couldn't rehearse with any of the other actors because they wouldn't be available until we started shooting. I was excited, making last-minute preparations, as the first day in front of the camera drew near, but one little script problem kept gnawing at me. In the movie, blood from a murderer's hands had been left on the keys of the pipe organ in the haunted house, and two delightful old ladies talk about it several times. One says, "There's still blood on the organ keys. They haven't been able to get it off." The other lady says, "And they used Bon Ami." I loved it. The problem seemed to be that our legal department had not been able to get a clearance from Bon Ami's legal department to use the name of their product. Every day I asked Montagne, "Any word from the legal department? Did we get clearance from Bon Ami yet?" The answer was always no. Three days before our start date, I asked Ed, "Do you mind if I call Bon Ami myself?" He said, "Go ahead." I went to my office and called Bon Ami. I asked if I could speak to their president, and I was delighted when he came right on the line. I explained how we wanted to use the name of his product, and he laughed, and said, "Sounds terrific! Please use it." Thus we saved the delightful "Bon Ami" line and I learned a valuable lesson. Never wait for legal departments. 147

The Shoot

I was plenty nervous when I drove onto the lot for our first day of shooting. I had a lot of eggs in this basket. As the day went on, I began to breathe a lot more easily. The actors seemed well prepared, and Alan was nothing short of brilliant. As we continued on into our first week, I felt almost jubilant. I was enjoying myself. I knew we had a good script and it was coming to life even better than I had hoped. Alan kept things moving along at a pretty good clip. We worked some pretty long days and nights and, miraculously, we came in on time. We actually shot our last scene at the end of the seventeenth day. Looking back on it, I wonder if the studio actually expected us to come in on schedule. In any case, I went home and slept for days. I had pulled a muscle in my leg in a scene running down the stairs in the haunted house, but I was otherwise in good shape. Just exhausted. For the first time in my career, during shooting, I had watched the dailies. The dailies are when the footage shot the day before is shown. I guess I was becoming experienced enough to be able to watch myself on-screen with some degree of objectivity. This is not an easy thing to do. The first few times you see yourself on-screen you want to throw up or something. In any case, I sat with Ed and the film editor while they discussed various shots. Occasionally, I offered my opinion although I doubt if they paid much attention. I became fascinated with editing and after the filming, I visited the editor occasionally while he was putting the picture together. I didn't dare see the rough cut! The rough cut is the first version of the entire movie, but without music and fades. It's not an easy thing to watch.

The court scene from *The Ghost and Mr. Chicken*

The First Looks

I waited anxiously for the finished product, and finally the day came. Ed called and told me the final print was in, and the following afternoon, Ed and Alan and I sat down in a screening room and watched *The Ghost and Mr. Chicken*. As we sat there watching the finished film unfold, my emotions are hard to describe. I had thought this would be fun, but I soon said to myself, You know what? It really isn't fun. When you've lived with a movie through its various stages the way we had, I realized it was impossible to be totally objective. The three of us sat there in deafening silence. When it was over, we went outside and stared at each other for a minute or two. Finally, Ed said, "I think it's a damn good picture. It just needs an audience." "Yeah, that's right," Alan said, "it needs an audience." "Right," I echoed. But as I got into my car to drive home, I thought, I don't know what it needs. For all I know, the audience will walk out after the first ten minutes!

The First Audience

The picture was scheduled to be released in about three months, so there was nothing to do but wait and see. Universal decided to give it a sort of premiere opening in New Orleans. They asked me to go down there and ride in a parade and make a brief appearance on the stage of the Joy Theater. Shortly before the opening, they sneak-previewed the picture in a movie theater in Hollywood. I slipped into the theater and took a seat in the audience and waited nervously. When the title *The Ghost and Mr. Chicken* came on the screen, my heart started pounding like a sledgehammer, but before long the audience began to laugh, and I felt a huge sense of relief. Nothing else, not at first, just relief. I watched and listened and they laughed pretty much at all the right places. Reaction was quite good, especially for a preview audience. Preview audiences are not usually terrific. After all, they're not fans. They didn't come to see this particular picture. Ed was right, it did need an audience. Sitting there watching it with a theater filled with people who had never seen it before and listening to their reaction brought the picture to life. It was a whole different movie than the one I had seen with Ed and Al at the studio that day.

The Opening

Ed Montagne went with me to New Orleans and we had a grand time. Ed acquainted me with oysters Rockefeller at Antoine's and we went to Pete Fountain's and did all the other good things New Orleans has to offer. I also worked very hard doing press interviews, and rode in the premiere parade.

The Joy Theater was packed for the opening, and I nervously took my seat in the audience. This was the real test. Thankfully, I experienced relief once more as the audience began to laugh. They were laughing so hard, in fact, that I had trouble hearing the dialogue. Then it occurred to me that the sound wasn't loud enough. This worried me, so I ran up to the projection booth and asked the projectionist to turn up the volume. He looked startled when I walked in, and not too pleased, but he turned up the sound. I finally went back to my seat and relaxed. When it was over, I was elated. It had gone better than I ever expected. The reviews were glowing the following day, and I was a happy man. The only thing marring my peace of mind on my way there was the fact that I had somehow developed a mild fear of flying. I have since overcome it completely, but it bugged me for several years. As I sat uncomfortably on the plane, noticing every little air bump we hit, I picked up a newspaper and began to read a story about an astronaut. I thought to myself, Now, if I were an astronaut sitting here, I wouldn't be the least bit nervous. Then I thought, Wouldn't it be funny if a guy somehow became an astronaut and he was afraid to fly? Then Jim Fritzell's acrophobia jumped into my mind. My God! What if the astronaut had acrophobia! I did a little double take. An astronaut with acrophobia! I couldn't wait to talk to Jim and Ev.

Time for TV

All five of my pictures at Universal took on pretty much the same operating procedure as *The Ghost and Mr. Chicken*. Universal decided to send me on the road with each picture to do PR. I usually went out for about three weeks. We wound up getting out one picture each year for the five years I was at Universal.

I kept a permanent office on the lot, but when I wasn't engaged in the filmmaking process, I had time to do other things. I continued to do guest shots on television shows, usually variety shows. I went back and did a couple of *Andy Griffith* shows. I kidded about how difficult it was to adjust to the "small screen."

After *The Ghost and Mr. Chicken* came out, I received an offer from CBS to do a television special for McDonald's. I think it was McDonald's first major television sponsorship. I asked Aaron Ruben to write and produce the show. We got Andy Williams and Juliet Prowse to be our guest stars. Aaron wrote a wonderfully funny show, and I had a great time doing it. I couldn't believe it, but once again I ran into a legal-department

My daughter, Karen, in a still from the *Don Knotts Variety Show.*

snag concerning the script when we were in preproduction. Aaron had written a very funny line in which columnist Ann Landers's name was used, and we had to get clearance from the legal department. A day or two before the taping, we still hadn't heard from legal. I was sitting in Aaron's office, telling him about my experience with Bon Ami. "I think I'll call Ann Landers," I said. Aaron said, "Go ahead." So I did. I got right through to her,

153

and when I told her the joke, she laughed, and said, "By all means, use it." Never wait for legal departments.

I worked with Juliet Prowse several times. I loved her. She was a great dancer and a great lady. In this particular show, she wore a costume that was just a little bit too skimpy for television in those days. It somehow got by Aaron, and when the CBS executives ran the show, they nearly fainted. They had the engineers fill the screen with haze and when it came out on television, you could hardly see poor Juliet through the smoke or mist or whatever it was. That really struck me as funny.

I did another special that season with Andy Griffith and Tennessee Ernie Ford. That was a blast! You'll never guess who one of the girls in our chorus line was. None other than Goldie Hawn. I remember Tennessee Ernie thought she was the cutest thing he had ever seen.

A Job in Jolly Old

During one of my free periods at Universal, a really interesting thing happened. An NBC executive called me into his office and asked me if I'd like to MC a TV variety show in London. "London, England?" I asked. "The one and only," he said. It was a show that was to be seen not only on NBC in this country but also in England and all of Europe. "You will, of course, have to perform one of your monologues, as well as MC," he said. When I look back on it now, I don't know how I had the nerve to say yes. First of all, I was completely unknown in England at that time, and second of all, I'd never hosted a TV variety show. But I had also never been to England, so I jumped at it!

When I landed at Heathrow Airport, I was excited. They put me up at the Savoy, no less, where I was treated like royalty. The producer visited me in my suite at the hotel and laid out the plans for the show. "Your guest artists will be Sir Robert Morley, Julie London, and a European musical group," he said. Wow! I was traveling in fast company. "A chorus line of young men and women who both sing and dance will open and close the show," he went on. "You will start things off with a few jokes, of course—" I interrupted, saying, "I don't exactly do jokes." He stared at me, then said, "Well, we do have to get the show on the road, now, don't we?" "I'll think of something," I muttered. I thought to myself, "Am I going to have trouble with this guy?"

I worried about the opening for a couple of days. Finally, an idea hit me. Something I had seen Jack Benny do made me think of it. I put together a routine where I stood in front of the chorus line, directing them to sway as I swayed while they sang. Then a young woman on the end began to sway out of sync. I halted the singing and walked over to her, and demonstrated the correct way to sway. She looked at me so sweetly that on impulse, I grabbed her and kissed her, then returned to center stage. I began directing the singing and swaying again, when a *guy* on the other end of the line started swaying out of sync. I looked helplessly at the audience, then walked reluctantly to him and showed him that he was swaying wrong. Then, smiling, he pushed his face toward me for a kiss. I abruptly rushed to the other end of the line and kissed the girl with full embrace.

I knew British audiences loved gay humor, and I thought they'd get a kick out of this. My hunch was right. The routine got screams. The whole show turned out to be a hit, in fact, and I returned to London several times over the next few years to do various television shows. I always enjoyed it.

In costume for *The Reluctant Astronaut*

The Reluctant Astronaut

When the decision was made to do *The Reluctant Astronaut* for my second picture at Universal, Ed Montagne requested permission from NASA to shoot some of our stuff at the Space Center in Houston and at Cape Kennedy in Florida. He thought he would be turned down, and he was looking at the

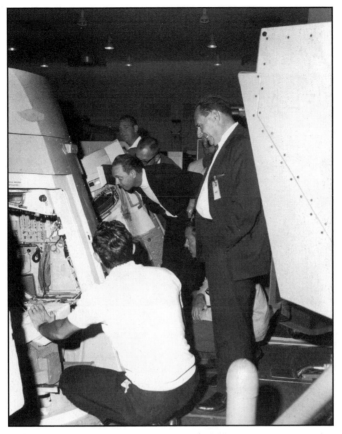

Ed Montagne and I tour the facilities at NASA

possibility of faking it at Vandenberg Air Base. Much to his surprise, NASA granted permission to shoot all we wanted at their facilities. As it turned out, they wanted all the publicity they could get.

When Jim and Everett and I sat down to do the script, we realized we would be writing about something we weren't familiar with, so Everett and I decided to fly to Cape Kennedy to have a look around. NASA gave us the VIP treatment. They showed

Everett Greenbaum and me

us everything there was to see at the Cape. A rocket was being readied for launch at the time, and much to our delight, they put us on the elevator and took us up to the capsule. It was quite an experience.

Once again I had a ball with Jim and Everett, and I was delighted with the script we came up with. Ed Montagne decided to direct this one himself. This time, they gave us all of twenty-three days to shoot the picture. Wow! I guess the success of *The Ghost and Mr. Chicken* made them magnanimous!

Nevertheless, the shooting went well. We got some great footage at NASA in Houston, as well as Cape Kennedy, and this time I was pleased with the final print, even when I saw it without an audience.

A sad thing happened, however, when I was on the road

Posing at Cape Kennedy

selling the picture. I was about to leave for the theater in Dallas to make an appearance when I got a call from my advance man informing me that NASA's first tragedy had struck. Three astronauts had been killed during a training exercise at the Cape. Universal thought it best to pull the picture and rerelease it at a future date. The movie lost its momentum, of course, but it picked up later on and did quite well. Like *The Ghost and Mr. Chicken,* I'm proud to say it has stood the test of time.

"This is the sort of thing that makes an astronaut reluctant in the first place."

Meeting with Arthur Godfrey in Florida

The Charm of Arthur Godfrey

During one of my hiatus periods at Universal, I costarred with Arthur Godfrey in a television movie written and directed by Hal Canter. Godfrey was one of the most fascinating people I ever met. To say that he had been a big star would be putting it mildly. In the early 1950s, Godfrey had three half hours of evening TV, all of which ranked in the top five half hours of television prime time. Coupled with his daytime radio programs, CBS said Godfrey reached 82 million people a week. In 1954, his combined broadcasts pulled in 12 percent of CBS's network revenue. CBS had a vice president in change of Godfrey. He was that important.

It's hard to say exactly what made Godfrey so popular. He strummed a ukelele and sang in a nasal tone, but mostly he just talked and charmed.

He charmed everyone, particularly the ladies. Women loved him. He was also a wonderful interviewer, one of the best.

Interviewed by Arthur Godfrey

I had met Godfrey some years earlier at a press junket for *The Incredible Mr. Limpet* in Weeki Watchee, Florida. He had recorded one of the songs from *Limpet,* and he agreed to come down and interview the actors, and, of course, plug his record. Sammy Fain had written some beautiful music for *Limpet*, and Godfrey recorded a cute song called "I Wish I Were a Fish," which I sang in the movie. While we were there, he arranged a time for me to come to New York City and be a guest on his radio show. This was in the sixties, and his star had faded somewhat, but he still had a major radio following. He had a full orchestra and singers, and he was still a pretty big deal.

I had heard a lot of stories about temperamental stars, but I had never actually seen any real displays of temperament until the day I did Godfrey's show. The show was recorded for a later date, and Godfrey wore earphones during the broadcast. Suddenly, in the middle of the show, he pulled off his earphones and threw them on the floor as hard as he could. "Goddammit, CBS!" he screamed. "When are you going to get me a decent pair of earphones?" And he marched angrily back and forth muttering epithets. The announcer stepped up quickly, pulled off his earphones, and said, "Use mine, Arthur, use mine." It was a tense moment. The band and singers sat dead still. Then within two or three minutes, as suddenly as the outburst had begun, it was over, and Godfrey was oozing with charm again.

When I worked with him in Canter's movie, I found him to be delightful company. When the tours came through Universal, most actors ignored them. Not Godfrey. He stopped and chatted with them and flattered the ladies every chance he got.

I enjoyed making the film with Godfrey. I had heard all the stories about how mean he could be when he was at the top, and I had seen a display of his temper, but I liked him. You just couldn't help liking the guy.

The Third Picture

The story for my third picture was supplied by the studio. Universal owned a western called *Paleface*, which had starred Bob Hope and Jane Russell. The studio felt the story was perfect for me. It was about a dentist who went out to the old West to practice his dentistry, and got himself in all kinds of trouble with gunrunners and Indians and a pistol-packing Annie Oakley.

The Shakiest Gun in the West

164

Barney Fife and Other

Posing as a squaw in
The Shakiest Gun

Once again, Jim and Everett and I sat down in my office to go to work. We used the basic story, which was a good one, but we wrote an entirely different picture. We called it *The Shakiest Gun in the West*. I really had fun shooting this picture. I love working in westerns. Getting dressed up like a cowboy and tramping around on western streets makes you feel like a kid again. Ed Montagne hired Alan Rafkin to direct again.

The Shakiest Gun in the West

Just One of Those Days

One day during the shoot, Alan and I were having lunch in my trailer, which was parked on a western street in Universal's back lot, when we thought we smelled smoke. I opened the door and was greeted with flames about two stories high right across the street. Two or three houses on that side of the street were on fire. We, of course, lit out of there, and joined dozens of actors and crew people who were wasting no time getting to

Barbara Rhodes played my sweetheart in _The Shakiest Gun in the West_

safety. When we were out of the area, we stopped and watched the fire, which looked like it was consuming Universal's entire western section. Pretty soon the fire trucks began to arrive. Then, all of a sudden, here came Lou Wasserman. He hurried past us and ran down to the edge of the fire. You could see him down there, pointing and charging around, and talking to the firemen. After a while, he came walking slowly back toward us. This man who usually looked full of confidence and on top of the world was now walking with his head down and a defeated look in his eyes. When he got almost to us, I couldn't help it, I said, "Well, Mr. Wasserman, it looks like it's just gonna be one of those days." Lucky for me, he grinned.

The Shakiest Gun in the West

Sparring with the Champ

While I was in Houston, Texas, doing PR for *The Shakiest Gun in the West*, Muhammad Ali was in town training for his next fight. This gave our PR man an idea for some publicity. He asked Muhammad's people if Muhammad would consider posing for some pictures, sparring around with me with the boxing gloves on. Much to my surprise, Muhammad said okay. The next afternoon, we went over to his quarters and took the pictures. I enjoyed doing it. He was a lot of fun. I told him I was going to say a few words onstage that night before my movie, and I invited him to come on over and see it. He said, "I'll do that. I'll bring my friends." I said, "Say, do you want to come up onstage with me and spar around? We could get some fun out of that." He said, "Let's do it. I'll be in the audience. You introduce me."

Muhammad had recently become a Muslim and had changed his name from Cassius Clay to Muhammad Ali, but the news hadn't gotten to me yet. So when I introduced him onstage

Comparing muscles with Muhammad Ali

that night, I called him Cassius Clay. I gave him a big buildup, then said, "Come on up here, Cassius." The audience applauded and applauded and I waited and waited, but he didn't come up. Then I heard my PR man in the wings calling in a desperate stage whisper, "Muhammad Ali! His name is Muhammad Ali." So I said, "Come on up here, Muhammad Ali," and up he came. We put on the gloves and sparred around and got a lot of laughs. I ran into Muhammad several times after that, and he always greeted me like an old friend. What a spectacular man he is!

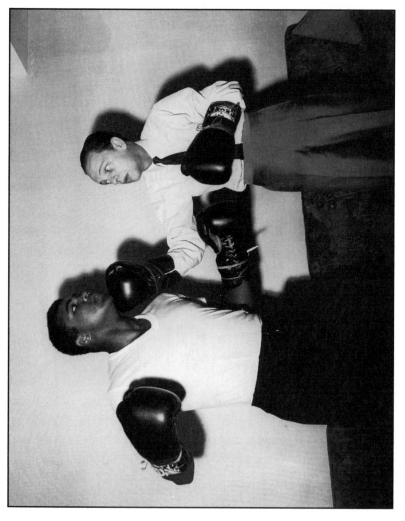

I told Ali everything I know

Barney Fife and Other (

Staring down Ali

Nat Hiken Comes to Town

The *Shakiest Gun in the West* was a hit. It was doing well at the box office and the critics were praising it. Even *Time* magazine! They ran a picture of me with a good review. That was three hit pictures in a row. I don't mean monumental hits, but they were successful. They made money. Just as I was beginning to feel somewhat secure about my career in features, however, clouds began to form on the horizon.

For openers, Jim and Everett were not available to write my next picture. Fritzell did give me a notion for one, though. It was a spoof on Hugh Hefner and *Playboy* wherein, almost by accident, I would become a Hefneresque editor.

My son and daughter cut up on the set of *The Shakiest Gun*

Along about this time I heard that a top comedy writer, Nat Hiken, had just moved to the West Coast from New York. Nat was one of the most highly respected comedy writers in the business. He had been the head writer for such great comics as Milton Berle and Fred Allen. His most recent television successes had been *Sergeant Bilko,* starring Phil Silvers, and *Car 54, Where Are You?* He had written and produced both these shows. I had heard by way of the grapevine that Nat was looking for a project, so I decided to give him a call. He accepted my invitation to lunch and we met the following day at the Brown Derby in Hollywood. When I told him the idea Jim had given me, he flipped. "My God,

Barbara Rhodes and me

that's great!" he said. "Let's do it." And the next thing I knew he was in an office at Universal writing the screenplay. He also made a deal with Universal within days to direct to the picture as well. I could see that Nat was not one to let a whole lot of grass grow under his feet.

This time, I was to have nothing to do with the writing. Nat worked alone, and that was just fine with me. He was a tireless worker. He was in his office at least ten hours every day. Nat claimed that writing was mostly rewriting, and I soon found out he wasn't kidding. Every once in a while, he would call my office, and say, "Don, I've got some pages I want you to read. Come by tonight and pick them up before you go home." After I'd read the pages, I'd drop by his office the following day. I'd say, "Nat, the pages were great." "Oh," he'd say, "I'm sorry, I rewrote those already." That happened three or four times and I finally decided it might be best just to wait until he had a final screenplay ready to turn in. He told me he once wrote a sketch for a television show, and after it was performed, he went home and rewrote it.

Nat and Jackie Gleason

Nat and Ed Montagne usually had lunch together at the commissary. I joined them whenever I could because Nat was a great raconteur. He kept us entertained with fascinating show biz tales. One day, he told us a story concerning Jackie Gleason and himself that I will never forget.

Around 1950, although Jackie Gleason as yet had no national presence, he was beginning to build a name for himself on the nightclub circuit. Finally he got a good break in New York. He landed a starring role in a Broadway revue called *Along Fifth Avenue*. Nat was writing for *The Fred Allen Radio Show* at the time, but he wrote a couple of pieces for this revue. One was a number for Jackie Gleason called "The Foreign Legion."

When the revue was in out-of-town tryouts in New Haven, Connecticut, Nat drove up to see the show. While he was there, Gleason hit him up for twenty dollars. Nat was the first to admit that he was not what you would call "easy with a buck," but he peeled off the twenty. "Thanks, pal," Jackie said, "I'll pay you back when we open in New York." What Nat didn't know was that Jackie owed everybody in town.

The show was a big hit and at the cast party, Nat sidled up to Jackie, and said, "How about that twenty I lent you in New Haven?" Jackie said, "Come on, Nat, give me a chance to get on my feet. Catch me later." When the revue finally closed, Nat still hadn't heard from Jackie. At the closing party, once again Nat went to Gleason and asked him for the money, and once again, he was given the runaround.

Sometime thereafter, the Great One signed a one-million-dollar contract for *The Jackie Gleason Television Show*. There was a huge celebration party, and again, here came Nat asking

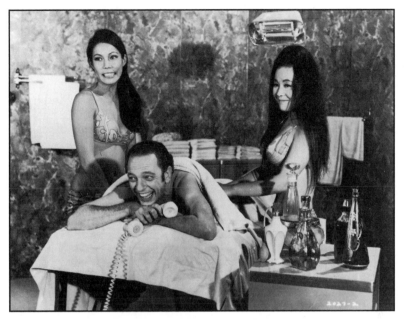

I get a good rubdown on the set of *The Love God*

Jackie for the twenty. Jackie cracked, "Who carries that kind of small change?"

Several years later, Jackie's manager, Bullets Durgam, called Nat and asked him to lunch. Durgam said to Nat, "Listen, Jackie's gonna play Las Vegas and he wants to use the 'Foreign Legion' number you wrote for him in *Along Fifth Avenue*. What do you want for it?" Nat said, "I'd be glad to talk about it, but first I want Jackie to pay me the twenty he owes me." Durgam reached into his pocket. "Twenty dollars? Here." "No, no," said Nat, "I want a personal check from Jackie Gleason, signed by Jackie Gleason. When I get the check, then we'll talk."

They met about a week later and Bullets reached into his pocket, hauled out a crumpled check with Jackie's signature, and handed it over. Nat looked at it for a long time. Finally he said,

Doris Day and me in _Move Over Darling_

"Okay, Bullets, I said when I got the check I'd talk, and I'm talking. The 'Foreign Legion' number is not for sale!"

No more than four weeks later, I was having lunch with my secretary, BJ, in a Hollywood restaurant, the Villa Capri, when who should walk in but Jackie Gleason and his famous secretary, Honey. After a while, a waiter came over and told me Jackie wanted us to join them for a drink. I was terribly flattered when Gleason said, "You know, you work just like me, from the inside out. From a character." I was flattered to know that anybody that big even knew I existed. He asked me what I was doing, and I told him I was about to shoot a picture called *The Love God*. Like any good comedian, Jackie wanted to know who wrote it. "Nat Hiken," I told him. "Oh," he said, "he's the greatest, the greatest!" Then after a pause, he said, "By the way, if you ever get a chance, will you ask Nat if a number called 'The Foreign Legion' is available?"

I never did get a chance to work with Gleason, but I did work with his *Honeymooners* sidekick, Art Carney. Art and I did a limited engagement of *The Odd Couple* at the Arlington Park Theater in Chicago. Art had played the part of Felix on Broadway, and he wanted to switch and do Oscar. So I played Felix. I had a great time. Art is a funny guy and a wonderful actor.

The Love God

Because of my three box office hits, coupled with the stature of Nat Hiken, Universal decided to put a little more money into *The Love God*. They brought in a name, Ann Francis, to play my leading lady. And of all things, they gave us a six-week shooting schedule. As was his custom, Nat worked tirelessly as a director, and we had to keep pace. Nat became totally absorbed in his work. He told me that when he came to the end of the season one year on the *Bilko* series, he became aware that he hadn't been feeling well, so he finally went to the doctor. After an examination, the doctor said, "Nat, you are getting over hepatitis."

The Love God

Nat brought the picture in on time and everything looked rosy, but I was in for a couple of jolts. When the studio tried to book *The Love God,* they learned that they had miscalculated. Remember, my first three films were G-rated family pictures. *The Love God* had just a tinge of the naughty in it, and it was given an M rating. M stood for "mature audiences" in 1970. Even though the sexual revolution was in full swing and people were taking their clothes off right and left in movies, people apparently did not want to see me in anything but clean family pictures. Universal had trouble booking *The Love God.* I'm not sure how many, but I heard that a great number of theaters turned the picture down. In any case, it did not do well at all.

Bob Sweeney

But the worst news of all came when, a few weeks after we finished the picture, I received a phone call informing me that Nat Hiken had died from a heart attack. I couldn't believe it! Nat was only in his middle fifties. What a tragic loss to the world of comedy. I felt so privileged to have known and worked with this talented man.

A Triumphant Special

During the next break in my schedule at Universal, CBS offered me a deal to do another special. Aaron Ruben wasn't available this time, so I asked Bill Dana to help me write it. Bill and I came up with what I thought was a brilliant idea. In view

Elaine Joyce

of the fact that movies and theatrical productions were running amok with nudity and blue material, we decided to call our show *The Don Knotts Nice Clean Decent Wholesome Hour,* wherein I showed comedically what a tough job I had trying to sell a clean show "in this day and age." It had a good theme, and Bill and I came up with some very funny stuff. But about halfway through the script, we ran into a block and couldn't seem to finish it. I went to Nick Vanoff, who was to produce the show, and he put two of his writers on it, Frank Peppiat and John Aylesworth. I couldn't believe what a great job these two guys did with the rest of that script. It was absolutely marvelous. Apart from *The Andy Griffith Show,* I think that special was one of the best things I ever did on television. It was timely, unique, and very funny. I was very disappointed when CBS decided to run it on a Friday night. Although it did win its time slot, that's not a good night to pick up a big viewing audience, and the show went largely unnoticed. At least that's what I thought at the time.

Picture Number Five

When it came time to do a fifth picture at Universal, even though the climate was not good for family pictures, the studio insisted we give it another try. Ed Montagne and I started looking for another story idea. Once again, Jim and Everett were not available, so Ed and I sat down and wrote a treatment for a picture we decided to call *How to Frame a Figg*. Ed hired a writer named George Tibbles to write the first draft. Ed and I wrote the second draft, and Jim and Everett agreed to come in and do a final polish. Universal signed Elaine Joyce to be my leading lady. We shot the picture in five weeks. It wasn't the greatest movie script ever written, but I thought it turned out to be a pretty funny little picture. It still shows up on television once in a while. But alas, it did not do very well at the box office. People had simply stopped going to family movies.

A Tough Season

I said the *Don Knotts Nice Clean Decent Wholesome Hour,* which was done for CBS, went largely unnoticed, but apparently NBC did notice it. Shortly after we filmed *How to Frame a Figg,* Sherwin called and said that Mort Werner, then president of NBC, had loved the special and wanted to talk to me about doing a weekly variety series. I was in shock. I had never entertained the notion of hosting a variety series even in my wildest dreams. I demurred, but Sherwin insisted I have a drink with Mort.

I said to Mort Werner, "Look, I spent six months gathering the material for that show. Coming up with a script for a variety hour every week is an entirely different story. Besides, hosting a variety series is not really my bag." But Mort persisted, and in the end, he made me an offer I couldn't refuse. Before I knew it, I was staring at a season of twenty-two variety shows in it, and I was sorry I had given in. For the first time in my career, I felt I was up against something I could not handle.

For openers, I couldn't deal with writers firing that many sketches at me every week. I couldn't seem to make decisions on material that fast. I was used to working more slowly, more thoroughly. We were able to get great guest stars, the best. People like Bill Cosby, Steve Allen, Bob Newhart, Jimmy Durante, Raymond Burr and, in one show, the whole Bridges family—Lloyd, Jeff and Beau. But we still limped along in the ratings. On top of everything else, the variety show competition was fierce that season. I can't recall how many, but there were a number of variety shows on the air.

Occasionally, a special guest star would bump us up a notch or two in the ratings. Two stars who did that for us were Bill

Cosby and Jimmy Durante. I got Bill Cosby to do the show myself. Not only did he say okay but he did the show twice. My God, what a powerful entertainer that man is. He came up with wonderful sketch ideas, and we had the audience eating out of the palms of our hands. Typical of the way his mind works, in a pantomime sketch we did of two guys playing chess, Cosby had the prop people make one of my pawns out of chocolate. When his rook took my pawn, he just popped the pawn in his mouth and ate it. What a huge laugh that simple joke got. I did enjoy doing the two shows with Bill.

Jimmy Durante was also a real kick to work with. Audiences were crazy about Jimmy. When you were on stage with him, you could just feel the love pouring out from the audience. It was uncanny. He was such a cute guy. I had a funny experience with Jimmy a few years down the road. Jimmy and I were hired by Smith-Hemion Productions to cohost a *Kraft Music Hall* TV special. At our first meeting with Smith and Hemion, Dwight Hemion said, "Because of the image that you two fellows project, we thought it would be cute if, instead of a line of chorus girls, we use kids." I looked at Jimmy. He nodded slightly, but he seemed to have nothing to say. When Jimmy and I got outside after the meeting, Jim grabbed my arm, and said vehemently, "Hey, Don! No little kids! We want broads!" And he stormed down the street. The "kids" idea was soon dropped and Jimmy got his "broads!"

I'll never forget an amusing incident that occurred with Jimmy during rehearsal for that show. When we were introduced, I was to enter from stage right and Jimmy from stage left. We were told they wanted both of us to do Jimmy's strut (for which he was famous) as we walked on stage. In other words, the director said, "Jimmy, you do yourself, and Don, you do Jimmy." I was waiting on my side of the stage during dress rehearsal when we were told we would have to wait for a light to be fixed. A minute or two later, Jimmy's face peeped at me from around a curtain and in a plaintive voice, he said, "Hey, Don, do me! I don't know what I do!"

It Finally Ends

At midseason, we brought in Bob Sweeney, who was between directorial assignments, to see if he could breathe some new creative energy into the show. Bob made some personnel changes in the writing staff, and created a couple of new segments in the show, one of which was a running sketch that took place in a library. He cast Gary Burghoff, of *M*A*S*H* fame, to support me in this department. These changes improved the show somewhat, but we still showed no significant gain in the ratings. As the season ground into its final weeks, I was becoming exhausted. When we came to our last hiatus week, I decided to go to Hawaii. I fell asleep the minute I sat down on the plane, and I did not wake up until we landed in Honolulu. When I arrived at my hotel room, I fell asleep again, and except for an hour here and there to eat some food, I slept the entire week. I might as well have stayed home. The season finally came to an end, and I licked my wounds and went home for a long rest.

The rest, in fact, was a little too long for comfort. My show's failure had put my name on the back burner, and it was a good three months before my phone rang again.

Kay and I had divorced during the Universal days, and it was during the respite, following my variety show, that I met and eventually married Loralee Czuchna.

Back to the Boards

I began to wonder if my career was really over. When my phone finally did ring again, it was from an unexpected source. A young man named Jim Burrows, now one of the biggest directors in television, wanted to know if I would be interested in starring in a play called *Last of the Red Hot Lovers,* by Neil Simon, in a little theater in San Diego. I hadn't done anything in legitimate theater since *No Time for Sergeants.* A friend of mine, Sandra Giles, and I drove down to San Diego to look the theater over. It was a tiny house called the Off-Broadway Theater, and it didn't pay much money, but I decided to give it a whirl. Hey, I wasn't working! It turned out to be a good decision. We were a hit and God knows I needed a hit along about then. When we closed, Sherwin managed to get us booked into the Huntington Hartford Theater, now the Doolittle Theater, in Hollywood. Like many motion picture and television actors, I have sandwiched theater engagements into my schedule ever since.

Over the next three or four years, my career went what you might call sideways. I did a lot of theater and a lot of guest shots on television, mostly variety shows and specials, but I wasn't moving onward and upward.

The cast of *The Odd Couple*

Bob Hope and a Cue Card Miscue

Bob Hope began calling me periodically to do his TV show. That was a real kick. I had always been a big fan of Hope. One of the most unusual experiences I had working for Hope was on a special he did on a navy battleship, tying in his visit with servicemen, as he often did, though it was in the 1970s and there was no war at the time.

Bob used cue cards for everything, and since you did dozens of jokes and got no more than one or two rehearsals, nobody tried to learn anything. When we rehearsed our big sketch the day before the show, there was a slight mishap in the cue card de-

The cast of *Mind with a Dirty Man*

partment. The fellow holding my cards was apparently new, and he was slow at pulling them, causing me to hesitate while he cleared the next card. Hope, who was usually so lovely to work with, suddenly became quite upset with me. He said, "Don, you're stumbling over this stuff! You'd better go over these lines tonight!" I tried to explain, but he would have none of it. *His* cards, of course, were pulled on time. After he left, I walked over to Barney McNulty, the king of all cue cards in Hollywood, and told him what happened. "Don't worry," Barney said, "we'll have an experienced guy on your card tomorrow."

When we did the show, Barney's cue card guy pulled my cards with precision, and I did my lines without a hitch. The sketch played like a house on fire and when I came out to take my bow, Hope walked over to shake my hand. With a big, wide grin on his face, he said, "Studied, didn't you?"

Groucho

If you grew up when I did, you just had to be a huge fan of the Marx brothers. Groucho, of course, was the ringleader and he was one of the funniest men that ever stopped in front of a movie camera. I never got to work with Groucho, but I did bump into him occasionally, and he always came up with a line or two that made me laugh. His wit was amazing. One day, I walked into a doctor's waiting room and there sat Groucho, cornered by a female fan who didn't want to leave him alone. Suddenly she recognized me, and said, "Why, you're Don Knotts." Groucho said, "He's always known that." Finally I asked Groucho, who was getting a little long in the tooth by then, if he was working on anything. "Who has time to work?" Groucho shot back. "From here I go to my urologist. From my urologist, I go to my cardiologist. From my cardiologist, I go to my dermatologist. From my dermatologist, I go to my . . ." I was still laughing when the door opened and the nurse admitted Groucho.

Golf—A Laughing Matter

Forget my nervous character and Barney Fife. A lot of my friends think the funniest thing about me is my golf game. Ask Bob Newhart or Don Rickles. One day, when I was playing with Bob and Don, I stubbed an eight-iron shot so badly that it raised a huge cloud of dust engulfing the three of us. Coughing, Rickles shouted, "Look at that! When Knotts hits a golf ball, it's like a grenade went off!"

Speaking of Rickles, he really cracked me up one day during an *Andy Griffith* rehearsal. Don was doing a guest shot on the show, and as his career was just beginning to climb, he was anxious to do his best. Around four in the afternoon, Andy said, "Well, I think we've rehearsed enough, let's go home." "No, come on," Don said anxiously, "Let's rehearse some more. Sure, you guys have got millions of feet on film. All I've got are home movies of me and my cousin on the swing."

Even *I* find my attempt to play golf amusing, but why I continue to be a duffer is beyond my comprehension. I pay close

Always working on my golf swing

attention to the good golfers and do my best to emulate them. I even use the same foul language they use, but nothing helps. (I think my friend Tom Poston, though, has the best golf-course foul language I've ever heard. His epithets are legendary.) Nevertheless, I do enjoy playing, and I have many pleasant memories associated with the game of golf.

The Nixon Incident

One of my most extraordinary golf experiences occurred back in the 1960s. An NBC executive whose name I can't recall, Sherwin Bash, and I were about to tee off at the Bel Air Country Club, when the starter shouted, "Hold it, fellas, Dick Nixon wants to join you." I thought to myself, "Dick Nixon? I don't know any Dick Nixon." Then I looked up and here came *the* Richard Nixon trotting down the hill toward us. He had just lost the gubernatorial election in California, and I guess he wanted to cool off. Mr. Nixon and I became partners, and we set up some small bets, and as I recall, we did win a few bucks. It was at lunch in the Grill Room after golf when a most interesting conversation took place. Mr. Nixon was telling us how he intended to retire from public life and practice law in Los Angeles when the subject of restaurants came up. He said he was looking for some good eatery recommendations in L.A. "When I'm in New York," he said, "I usually have dinner at Pavillon. That place is very hard to get into." He went on, "But they usually give me a table because . . ." Then after a pause, almost as if he was about to announce something we didn't know, he said, "I used to be the vice president." There was a long pause, and I almost said, "You've got to be putting us on."

A Month with Orson Welles

One day, I got a call from the office of Bill Persky and Sam Denoff wanting to know if I would be interested in playing the part of the doctor in a television version of *The Man Who Came to Dinner* starring Orson Welles. Persky and Denoff had adapted the play for television and were producing it for Hallmark. Orson Welles, who lived in Paris at the time, was apparently having some tax difficulties with the IRS and did not want to return to the United States to do the show, so it was to be televised in England. Would I be interested? I would have paid *them* to do it.

We rehearsed the show for three weeks in London, and taped it over a period of three days in Southampton. These weeks were among my most memorable experiences in show business. For openers, how's this for a cast? Orson Welles, Joan Collins, Lee Remick, Marty Feldman, Mary Wicks (she originated the part of the nurse on Broadway), plus several British actors well known in England. We rehearsed in a hall not far from Harrod's department store, and the first three or four days went along smoothly with an air of joviality. Orson Welles was a great raconteur, and he entertained us each morning with hilarious stories about famous people he had known all over the world. Welles enjoyed his own stories as much as his audience and his rich laughter echoed through the hall. He took a liking to me for some reason, and when he found out I was interested in magic, he was delighted. Welles was an accomplished magician. I had seen his magic act when he guested on *The Steve Allen Show*. Before he would sign to do his Shakespeare readings, he had insisted he be given a spot to do his magic act as well. Strangely enough, I never even met Welles when he did *The Steve Allen Show*. He did not mingle with the cast during rehearsals, and he seemed, in fact, quite unapproachable. But now in rehearsals for *The Man Who Came to Dinner*, he regaled me with stories about Houdini, whom he had met through his father when he was a kid. Yes, the first two or three days of rehearsal sailed breezily along, and Orson Welles worked happily, kidding with his cast, and having only an occasional glass of wine, supplied by his personal secretary. But this heady fun was about to come to an end.

As we went off script (that is, when the actors are expected to know their lines), Welles's manner began to change. His face took on an anxious look, and he demanded that someone be brought in to hold cue cards for his lines. He also began to drink more wine, which he hid, unsuccessfully, in a coffee cup. He began to show signs of being slightly drunk, and he soon demanded that two more people be hired to hold cue cards so that he would always have his lines in his line of sight. It soon became clear to me that the poor man was scared to death. The part he was playing, that of Sheridan Whiteside, is a demanding role with thousands of lines housed in dozens of long speeches. At this point in his career, Welles had not played a part this big in several years.

He began to fight with the director, Buzz Kulik, and two or three times, Buzz stormed out of the rehearsal hall, vowing never to return. Welles demanded more and more cue cards, and before long, a dozen or so girls holding cue cards surrounded the rehearsal hall.

Through it all, for some strange reason, Welles held on to me as his one friend in the entire company. One afternoon, I was absent from rehearsal while I took my required insurance physical for the production, and when I returned, I learned that Welles had been very unhappy that I wasn't there. He had kept shouting, "Where is Don? Where the hell is Don?" Buzz Kulik called me aside, and said, "Listen, I don't want you to leave this rehearsal hall ever again. Whether you have a call or not, you be here!"

By the time the end of the three-week rehearsal period drew near, the cast was in a state of frenzy, and to make things worse, a flu bug struck and several actors became ill. In the true spirit of "the show must go on," however, everyone continued working. Lee Remick had a terrible case of bronchitis, and whenever she went into a coughing spell, it seemed to infuriate Welles. He would glare at her.

My scenes were with Welles, and he called me aside and whispered directions to me. His suggestions were, of course, brilliant. Welles was a genius. There is not much question about that, and I felt honored to be the recipient of his personal direction. When rehearsals ended, we traveled to a studio in Southampton to tape the show. On the first day of taping, Mr. Welles arrived bright and early, sober as a judge, and full of vim and vigor! He was a whole new person. His demeanor was in sharp contrast to the cast, most of whom were either half-dead from the flu or totally exhausted from the tension of the London rehearsals. Welles, of course, had become quite heavy by then, and his first demand was that the air-conditioning be turned up. No matter how cold it got, he wanted it even colder. Soon our fever-ridden actors were bundled up in overcoats and mufflers waiting to go on. To the best of my knowledge, Welles did not touch a drop of wine during the entire three days of taping. The proceedings went fairly smoothly except for an occasional argument between Welles and Buzz. Poor Marty Feldman, who played the part of Banjo, was so sick he practically had to be carried from the hotel to the studio to do his scenes.

Just as he was about to tape my biggest scene, Buzz came out of the control room to have a word with Welles. They got into a terrible fight, and they began screaming at each other. Buzz stormed into the control room and Welles looked at me plaintively. Shaking his head, he said, "Don, we have no director." Then Buzz's voice came over the loudspeaker. "All right," he yelled, "let's tape this!" Oh, boy, I thought to myself, what a way to go into my biggest scene. Thankfully, it seemed to go off without a hitch.

Except for the long hours and the fact that the British crew almost refused to stay overtime on the last night to finish the show, the entire taping went off pretty much without incident. I flew home tired and happy. The mischievous Orson Welles, after all, was a legend, and it had been a fascinating learning experience. When I finally saw the show on television, I thought it was pretty good, and it certainly gave no hint of the troubles we had seen. Ain't show business wonderful?

The Norman Tokar Episode

Iwas doing a play in Chicago when I got word that Disney wanted me for a picture. Well finally, I thought to myself! I had always thought I was Disney material. It wasn't Disney per se that wanted me, it turned out. It was a director named Norman Tokar, who was about to direct a picture for Disney called *The Apple Dumpling Gang*. It was a comedy western, and it teamed me up with Tim Conway. Tim and I had never worked together before, and I thought teaming us up was a stroke of genius on Norman Tokar's part.

Norman Tokar was not just a good director, he was excellent, but he could drive you crazy. He was slow and meticulous, and he did so many takes on every little scene that you wanted

With Tim Conway in *The Apple Dumpling Gang*

to kill him. He also spoke slowly, and it took him a long time to explain what he wanted. He had the patience of Job, and he certainly tested the patience of his actors, but he was good! He proved that to me with the job he did with *The Apple Dumpling Gang*. It was on the next picture I did for Norman that we had a little, what you might call, set-to.

It was a picture called *No Deposit, No Return*, in which I was costarred with David Niven, Darren McGavin, Herschel Bernardi, and Barbara Feldon.

When we started the picture in early June 1975, I told Norman that I had to start another project on August 15, and Norman said, "Don, you will be finished by six P.M. on August the fourteenth, I guarantee it." We were scheduled to finish a couple of weeks before that, but knowing how slowly Norman worked, I had to make sure.

We finished principal photography at the end of the first week of August, but I still had three or four shots left to do in coordination with my stuntman, so I was told to report to makeup at eight o'clock on Monday morning. I did so and wandered over to the sound stage. They were lining up some shots with the stunt people and the assistant director told me, "No, we won't get to you for a while. You might as well go back to your dressing room." I went back and read until lunchtime. After lunch, I went back to the sound stage. The AD said, "No, we won't get to you for a while yet." So I went back and read some more. At around 6:00 P.M., the AD called and said, "Why don't you go on home." "What about tomorrow?" I asked. "Norman wants you here at eight in the morning," he said.

Tuesday was a repeat of Monday. I was released at 6:00 and told to report at 8:00 A.M. again.

When the same thing happened on Wednesday, I was beginning to get a little steamed. There was no one to talk to and get it off my chest. All the other actors had been released. When I reported again on Thursday at 8:00 A.M. and was told that they weren't ready for me yet, I started to boil! Finally I called the sound stage. Through gritted teeth, I asked, "Is he getting close to needing me yet?" "Nope," came the answer, and something inside of me snapped. I don't usually go into rages, but I think I was in one that day. I ran as hard as I could from the dressing rooms to the sound stage. Norman was talking to the crew and the stuntmen when I hit the door. "You son of a bitch!" I yelled, and I started screaming at him. I don't even know what-all I said, but I remember telling him that above all else, I had to be out of here by 6:00 P.M. on the following night as promised. Norman finally said, "Now, calm down, Don. As a matter of fact, we're going to do a couple of your shots right now." We did the shots and Norman told me we had a couple more to do the next day.

When I got home that night, I felt guilty. I had never railed like that at a director in my entire life . . . and right in front of the crew. I was ashamed. Nevertheless, I returned the following day with head unbowed. Norman and I communicated normally during the day, and the incident seemed to be forgotten. By 5:00 P.M., it seemed to me that we had finished everything, but Norman appeared to be stalling. He wandered around with his cameraman for a while, and finally he called to me, "Don, remember that rope you had to hang from a couple of weeks ago? I need to get another angle on that." So I was hoisted up about two stories where the rope was fastened. Norman rolled the camera and I hung on that rope until I thought my arms would pull out of their sockets. Finally, while I was still hanging there, Norman yelled, "Don, it is exactly six P.M. on August the fourteenth, and that's a wrap! Let's go home, boys." And with that, he marched out the door. Norman had the last laugh, no question about it! And I deserved it. A few weeks later, Norman invited me to dinner, and we both had a good laugh over it.

Teaming Up with Tim

There is absolutely no question about it—Tim Conway is one of the funniest performers in the business. The toughest thing about working with Tim is keeping a straight face. As in the case of Howard McNear, you were never quite sure what Tim was going to do when the camera turned on. I'm afraid I laughed into many a take. With Tim leading the way, we improvised most of our stuff in *The Apple Dumpling Gang*. Much to his credit, Norman Tokar did not pin us down with a lot of staging in our camera rehearsals. Most of the time he just turned us loose. We did a scene in which we sneaked a ladder out of the firehouse while the chief was sleeping, and wound up breaking a window in the building next door, which I hold to be as funny a piece of film as you will ever see. Norman gave us free rein and we ran with it. It was great fun!

As anyone who knows him personally will tell you, Tim is as funny off-camera as he is on. His running commentaries are brilliant. We did a lot of night shooting on *The Apple Dumpling Gang,* and my son, Tom, came out to the set almost every evening just to hear Tim's hysterical remarks while we sat around between takes.

I had to change my style a little when I worked with Tim. It was clear that Tim's character was the more ridiculous of the two, so I had to be the guy who at least thought he knew what he was doing, the take-charge guy.

Tim's comments are so unexpected they bowl you over. I remember once when we were shooting *The Apple Dumpling Gang Rides Again* on location in Canaab, Utah, the old man who drove us to the set each day was giving us a little local history. As we drove by a tiny airport, he said, "You know, back in the old days, the so-and-so Indians (I forget the tribe) up in Canada were running out of squaws, and they came down here looking for women." Tim said, "Man, that's a hell of a long way to go for a blind date." Laughing, the old man tried to finish. "Well," he said, "they settled right along in here." "Gee," Tim came back, "you'd think they would have settled a little farther from the airport."

The Apple Dumpling Gang was a very successful movie. It made a lot of money for Disney. A couple of years later, we made the sequel, *The Apple Dumpling Gang Rides Again,* but the script wasn't nearly as good, and the movie didn't do well. Tim and I did two more pictures as a team, both independents. One called *The Prizefighter*, which was shot in Atlanta, came up short, but another, called *Private Eyes*, was a pretty funny little picture, and it did quite well. We filmed *Private Eyes* in Asheville,

The Apple Dumpling Gang

Barney Fife and Other

North Carolina. Each of us became busy with our separate careers, and Tim and I never made another picture together beyond the four just mentioned. It's really kind of a shame. As I said earlier, I thought we made a good team, and I still get mail wanting to know if we have plans to make another picture together. Who knows? Maybe we will yet.

Following *The Apple Dumpling Gang*, I made five more features for Disney over the next four years, in which I got to work with some wonderful actors. Nobody gets rich working for Disney, but I had a lot of fun and some great experiences, including a trip to Paris and Monte Carlo to shoot some scenes for *Herbie Goes to Monte Carlo*, which costarred Dean Jones.

A Call from Three's Company

One day, Aaron Ruben called and told me he had gotten an okay from Fred Silverman, then president of NBC, to write a pilot script for me to star in a situation comedy series. He came up with a cute script about a veterinarian. I signed a contract with NBC, and we taped the show in beautiful downtown Burbank. Unfortunately, it didn't sell. Shortly thereafter, Sherwin called with astounding news. The producers of *Three's Company* had made an offer for me to play the new landlord on their hit series. This came right out of the blue. I was floored. *Three's Company* was a very funny show. It had been in the top ten during its two years on the air. The three in *Three's Company* were Jack Tripper, Chrissie, and Janet, played by John Ritter, Suzanne Somers, and Joyce DeWitt. Jack's pal, Larry, was

Interviewed by Dinah Shore

played by Richard Kline. Norman Fell had been playing the land-lord, Mr. Roper, but he and his TV wife, played by Audra Lindley, were leaving the show to star in a spinoff series. I was called to take Norman's place as the new landlord, Ralph Furley.

I was thrilled, but I approached the new challenge with some apprehension. In the first place, unlike *The Andy Griffith Show,* *Three's Company* was taped in front of an audience. I had not done any multicamera situation comedies apart from a couple of pilots and one appearance with Lucille Ball. I had, of course, done a lot of variety shows in front of an audience, but that too was a whole different can of worms. In the second place, I knew I was going to have to hold my own with a mighty competent young cast. John Ritter had already earned a reputation for being one of TV's fun-

The cast of _Three's Company_

niest men. Suzanne Somer's popularity had gone way over the top, and Joyce DeWitt's comedic abilities were highly respected. Richard Kline was no slouch himself. He could spar with the best of them. In short, my work was cut out for me, baby!

My First Show

I came under severe fire immediately. The first show of the season was built around the new character, Ralph Furley, and I was given about a thousand yards of dialogue. This kind of show puts an inordinate amount of pressure on the actors. With very little rehearsal under your belt, you are expected to go out there in front of an audience and hit your marks, and know your lines. Then during a dinner break, scenes that didn't work are usually rewritten, and you are expected to clear your mind of the old lines, and memorize the new ones for the second taping. It's positively terrifying. I think actors are among the bravest people on earth. Howie Morris was once asked what he used for motivation. "Fear!" Howie screamed. I laughed heartily at that, and then I thought, You know what? He's right. Most of us are terrified before we go on, and once on, we slowly work our way through our fear.

During rehearsals of my first show, everyone in the company was very nice and tried to make me feel comfortable. In

My first episode of *Three's Company*

spite of my nerves, I did enjoy myself. The first show went pretty well, I thought, except for the fact that during one of my big scenes, I went up in my lines and they had to stop the tape and feed me my speech. I was embarrassed to death. After two or three shows, I began to settle down and relax into the routine.

The Cast

I was becoming more and more impressed with the cast. These kids were sharp. Joyce DeWitt had the comedy timing of a seasoned veteran. As Chrissy, Suzanne Somers played the audience like a yo-yo, and not enough can be said about John Ritter. His range was astounding. He could do whatever the writers asked of him, from the subtlest joke to the broadest comedy pratfall. John is also a very fine actor as his performance in the motion picture *Sling Blade* will testify. Richard Kline was Mr. Reliable. You could always count on him to get his laughs or help you get yours.

An actress named Ann Wedgeworth was brought in to play a new character who was supposed to work into some kind of love interest for Ralph Furley. Ann was very good, but for some reason the character did not seem to work and was dropped after the first season.

Shortly after the beginning of my second season with *Three's Company*, a somewhat shocking thing happened. In a dispute over money, Suzanne Somers quite suddenly left the show. This

With Joyce DeWitt and John Ritter

Barney Fife and Other (

A very funny man, John Ritter

turn of events produced a temporary void, as well as shock waves of bad feeling in the company, but in due time, not one but two new talented actresses, Priscilla Barnes and Jenilee Harrison, joined the cast. Chrissie was missed for a while, of course, but the show had so many other qualities and so many other quality actors that it survived quite readily, proving once again that no individual performer is indispensable to any good show.

The loss of Suzanne from the cast may have turned out to

The entire *Three's Company* family

be my gain. Without the comical Chrissie to write for, the writers seemed to be giving me funnier stuff to do. I enjoyed playing Ralph Furley. It allowed me to go as broad as I wanted, complete with double takes and pratfalls. It was really a lot of fun.

Mickey, Bernie, and Dave

Three's Company was produced by Mickey Ross and Bernie West, whose producing and writing credits include *All in the Family* and *The Jeffersons*. Mickey and Bernie had at one time been a comedy team, known simply as Ross and West. They headed up a staff of absolutely brilliant comedy writers. Man, did these guys write funny stuff! It was a joy to read the script each week. Dave Powers directed *Three's Company*. Dave had a wry sense of humor, and he was a lot of fun to work for. I was told he had a good sense of humor, so on my very first day of rehearsal, I decided to put him on a little bit. I whispered my plan to Dave's script supervisor, Carol Summers, and she and the cast watched with anticipation. (Bear in mind that all lines are memorized on this kind of show.) Making an effort to put a serious tone in my voice, I said, "Oh, Dave, they told you about my TelePrompTer, didn't they?" His face flushed slightly. "What?" he asked. "My TelePrompTer," I said, "They told you that I would be using the TelePrompTer, didn't they?" The color drained from Dave's face. Finally he said, "I was not informed of this, no." I kept this going as long as I could until I finally broke down laughing. The cast chimed in, and Dave said, "You son of a bitch! I can see I'm in for trouble."

My Most Humiliating Moment

In all my years of acting, I've only missed one entrance, and it pains me to talk about it, but here's how it happened. I'm crazy about the game of baseball, and living in Los Angeles, quite naturally, I'm a big Dodgers fan. In 1981, the game that would determine whether or not the Dodgers would make it to the World Series was being played while we were taping a *Three's Company* show. I had the game on television in my dressing room and during our breaks I would run in and take a quick look at the

game. On about my fourth visit to the dressing room, the game grew so exciting that I became totally glued to the set, completely forgetting about *Three's Company*. Suddenly the door flew open and our stage manager appeared in the doorway. "Mr. Knotts," he announced, "I'm afraid you've missed your entrance!" I have never been more shocked in my life. They had actually had to stop tape in front of an audience because I hadn't shown up. Humiliated, I made my way sheepishly down to the stage. I have never felt smaller in my life. Mickey Ross is a nice guy, but he obviously is not a baseball fan. I heard him say, "I'll be *so* glad when the baseball season's over." It was my first and last missed entrance. I might add that the Dodgers did win the game, however, and you can bet I was in the stands at Dodger Stadium to watch them beat the Yankees in the World Series!

Barney Fife and Other

Ralph Furley

A Four-Day Week

During my first two seasons with *Three's Company*, we put in a full five-day week on each show. We worked the first three days in the rehearsal hall, then on Thursday we blocked positions for the cameras and wound up the day with a full dress rehearsal. We began the day around noon on Friday with a line rehearsal, and the afternoon was spent doing a run-through on camera and the shows were taped that night. This was a fairly relaxed schedule and gave us at least some feeling of being prepared. But during the third season, bowing to the request of John and the girls, they cut us to a four-day week, chopping off one of the days in the rehearsal hall. As I've already said, these kids were sharp and they felt they didn't need five days. I wasn't so sure about me. I'm a slow worker. Besides, I was about twenty years older than everybody else in the cast.

It sure did speed things up. We now had to spend our first day reading down the script, blocking our positions, and learning our lines that night for a run-through the following day. It was a hasty beginning to the week all right, but before I knew it, I had adjusted. What a departure this was from the old Mayberry days where we often logged a forty-five- or fifty-hour week. The two shows were entirely different, of course, and cannot be compared in any way.

We all enjoyed our reunion in *Return to Mayberry*

The Mayberry Reunion

At the end of my fifth season, the producers of *Three's Company* decided to take the show off the air. They said they had run out of plot ideas, and I'm sure they had made more than enough money. They'd had seven hugely successful top-ten seasons.

Once again, my phone stopped ringing, so I decided to get up a little concert act and hit the college circuit. I asked good ol' Bill Dana to help me put some material together, and over the next two years I played about twenty-five colleges.

Then one day I got a call from my old friend Andy Griffith. It seemed that a deal had been struck with CBS to shoot a *Mayberry Reunion* show. Viacom was to produce it, and Andy hired Bob Sweeney to direct. The script was written by Everett Greenbaum and Harvey Bullock. Jim Fritzell had died several years earlier. We shot most of it in a little town near Santa Barbara, California, called Los Olivos. It took us about four weeks, and I wouldn't have traded the experience for anything. What fun it was getting together with everybody again. It was a little like a class reunion. Everybody looked a little older, but nobody had changed all that much. It was a good script and we had a ball shooting it. Back at the hotel at the end of the last day, Bob Sweeney said to me, "Don, I think we've done a good thing." And indeed we had. The show broke some all-time ratings records and has been rerun dozens of times.

What a Country

Shortly after the *Mayberry Reunion*, I got a call from two writers who had been on the *Three's Company* staff, Martin Ripps and Joseph Staretsky. Martin and Joseph were producing a new television series for syndication called *What a Country*. It was a very funny show about a school for immigrants who were learning to become U.S. citizens. They asked me to join the cast in midseason to play the principal. The Russian comedian, Yakov Smirnov, was the only name they had when I came on board. It was really quite a cute show, and since it was holding its own in the ratings, we were quite sure it would be picked up for a second season. But alas, it was not. *What a Country* died on the vine and it really should not have done so.

Divorced again, it was during this time that I met a wonderful actress named Francey Yarborough with whom I now share my life. Francey and I enjoy working together, and she has appeared with me in several theatrical productions.

214

Matlock

With the cancelation of *What a Country*, once again I was waiting by the phone. It didn't ring very often. The fact is, I didn't do much of anything over the next couple of years. A voice-over here, a commercial there, that sort of thing. The closest I came to getting back on television was costarring with Karen Valentine and Jenilee Harrison in a pilot that we shot at MGM. It didn't sell. I wasn't having much luck with pilots. I had done four of them in my career, and not one of them had sold. While I was working at MGM, I did get a chance to visit with Andy Griffith. Andy was filming *Matlock* on the lot. I think this was *Matlock*'s second season, and Andy was enjoying tremendous success.

It must have been our meeting at MGM that started Andy thinking because a few days later, he called and told me he wanted to work me into *Matlock* as a regular. Wow, what a friend! I think he saw that things hadn't been going my way, and I suppose he also thought it would be fun for the two of us to work together again.

I appeared on the show three or four times a season over the next five years. I'm afraid I wasn't much help to the show. For one thing, we couldn't do much real comedy because *Matlock* was, after all, not a comedy show. It was fun, though, watching Andy in action as Matlock. He was a little more tense on the set than he had been on the old show, but as always, he was on top of everything. My appearances on *Matlock* ended when Andy got NBC to move his operation to Wilmington, North Carolina.

aracters I Have Known

Ted Turner and me

On the Road Again

was beginning to feel good about myself again, and I was getting requests to make personal appearances in different towns around the country, mostly in conjunction with Mayberry fan clubs and merchandising people. I dusted off my old college concert material and a writer named Ken Hecht helped me reshape it, and I was on the road again. I also started to do theater again. Sherwin called one day and told me that a packager in Indianapolis by the name of Bob Young wanted to put together a tour for Barbara Eden and me to do *Last of the Red Hot Lovers.*

I had had an amusing experience in connection with Bob

Young about twenty years earlier. Young's office had called and asked me to serve as toastmaster at a dinner for Bob Hope in Indianapolis on the eve of the Indy 500. I told them toastmastering wasn't down my alley, but they said, "Oh, you've got to do it. Bob Hope has requested you. He really wants you to do it." Well, I thought, if Hope really wants me to do it, I'll give it a whirl.

When I arrived at the banquet hall, I ran into Hope. I said, "Hi, Bob," and Bob said, "Hi, Don. What are you doing here?"

Barbara Eden and Francey and I did do a short tour with *Last of the Red Hot Lovers*. We played ten or twelve cities over a period of seven weeks and wound up the tour with a seven-week run at Harrah's in Atlantic City. I've done quite a lot of theater since, including two long runs at the New Theater in Kansas City in *Harvey* and *You Can't Take It with You*, where I played opposite a wonderful actress named Dodie Brown. My latest project was a role in a Gary Ross movie for New Line Cinema called *Pleasantville*.

It's been fifty years since I hit New York and as I've looked back on my career while writing this book, I realize how lucky I've been. But then, of course, I also had a lot of drive, and it does take that. I remember once I was talking with Andy about a young actor we thought had a lot of talent. I remarked that I thought he would make it someday. Andy said he didn't think so. "Why not?" I asked. "He doesn't have the drive," answered Andy. It does take drive, as well as luck and talent. In any case, it's been a lot of fun. But now, after fifty years, I sometimes think it's time to hang 'em up.

Wait a minute! Was that the phone?

Francey Yarborough and me